Justin, Heaven's Baby

Justin, Heaven's Baby

by Sharon Marshall

Beacon Hill Press of Kansas City
Kansas City, Missouri

Printed in the United States of America
ISBN:0-8341-0833-X

Cover Art: Crandall Vail

Permissions to quote from the following copyrighted versions of the Bible are acknowledged with appreciation:

The Living Bible (TLB), © 1971 by Tyndale House Publishers, Wheaton, Ill.

New Testament in Modern English (Phillips), revised Edition © J. B. Phillips 1958, 1960, 1972. By permission of the MacMillan Publishing Co., Inc.

Contents

Dedication

This book is lovingly dedicated to my sister Velda who laughed, cried, and believed with me; who was so willing to give of her time, energy, and money; and who stood by my side during the 4½ beautiful months of Justin's life.

This book is also my thanks to a multitude of friends and relatives who gave undying love and support through my difficult days and my happy days. Because of their kindnesses, I am now more able to give to others in need, for they showed me what Christian love was all about.

Introduction

Life in this part of the 20th century is in some respects more paradoxical than it has ever been before. Technology and affluence have brought the "good life" to many around the world. Yet the historic facts of human suffering and frustration are, if anything, highlighted in their dismal darkness by the bright skies of developing life-privilege and enjoyments against which they appear.

Sorrow and tragedy still present themselves as uninvited guests at the threshold of most individuals and families at one time or another. They invade, though resisted, and leave their signs of hurt and havoc on a life, a home, that did not suspect such an arrival but a few minutes before. How often the scars of that visit remain for a lifetime!

A bombardment of questions inevitably accompanies these unwanted times. "Why did it come?" "How could a good God allow such to happen?" "How on earth can I go on living with the memory and aftermath of this event?"

Arranging one's attitude toward suffering and developing a philosophy about suffering has therefore become a prime necessity in today's life. At one extreme is the philosophy that makes God responsible for "everything," and those espousing it would counsel, "Just accept it without question and expect that in reality it is good coming in disguise." At the other end of the spectrum is the alternative of fatalism, which sees neither order nor Providence in this world and counsels, "Keep a stiff upper lip," "Join the dog-eat-dog rat race," and

"Survive in whatever way you can." Pursuing this alternative some have turned to alcoholism, drugs, and suicide.

One's philosophy about and attitude toward suffering determines the quality of life with which he ultimately lives, the quality of hope with which he lives, the quality of poise with which he lives.

This book is the moving biography of one person's journey through incredible and compounded tragedy. Sharon Marshall was jostled unwillingly along a bitter path, and in the midst of unthinkable events sought answers with which she could survive her crashing uncontrollable storms. Reading this book and living these moments with her will evoke tears, but it will do far more than that. It will bring one's own urgent introspections into sharp focus. It is my hope the contents of this book will help the reader formulate a personal philosophy of suffering. Then when his own jarring storms come, he may move through them triumphantly into brighter, more stable tomorrows.

Sharon Marshall found her way through. Here she affirms faith's reality and survival. Here she helps uncover principles to which others can relate, however different their journey may be.

Referring to his suffering experiences in a World War II concentration camp, Victor Frankl said, "We who lived can remember the men who walked through the huts comforting others, giving away their last piece of bread. They may have been few in number, but they offer sufficient proof that everything can be taken from a man but one thing: the last of the human freedoms—to choose one's attitude in any given set of circumstances, to choose one's own way."

In a set of circumstances in which her own life might have disintegrated, the author of this book found not only survival, but also healthy new life through the unique support of love from people and God. God's grace was sufficient, but the author personally chose the attitude that placed her where that grace could be sufficient for her. I know. I watched her do it.

As has been the case throughout the centuries of time, God's promises proved true. Sharon Marshall affirms: ". . . and God—the God of integrity—*always* keeps His promises."

—ROBERT H. SCOTT
Orange, California

1

A Brand-new Life!

*To every thing there is a season, and a time to every
purpose under the heaven: a time to be born . . .*(Eccles.
3:1).

What a way to start life—as an April fool! Perhaps I
could have a 1-hour labor—but I never do things that fast. A
26-hour labor? Never!

It was late evening, March 31, and our "April fool" baby
was definitely on her way. We laughed, thinking, Our little
girl will just have to learn early in life how to give back in
equal measure what she receives for being an April fool. We
settled down for a short rest before the hard labor set in and
laughed at our child's dim lot in life!

As I anticipated our new arrival, my thoughts raced
backward. This had been such a tough year! The arrival of
our "little girl" marked a new beginning for us. We had hoped
she would be born on Gammy's birthday, but she evidently
had a mind of her own. Gammy, Jerry's vibrant Christian
mother, had gone to heaven just a few months earlier. Perhaps to have been born on her birthday would have been too
heavy a load to carry through life; perhaps we would have
tried to make her into a "little Gammy," stifling her right to
become her own person. Compared to April Fools' Day,
though, that didn't seem so bad! Again, we laughed, antici-
pating our strong-willed child.

And personally, this had been a really difficult year.

Shortly after I became pregnant, we learned that Jerry was an alcoholic. For the remaining seven months, we were in counseling, battling this problem, sometimes making headway and sometimes moving backward. We lived in the wake of the financial disaster that alcoholism brings. In my mind I felt the arrival of our baby would signify the beginning of the end of that battle—a new lease on life. I had thought so many times, The baby has to be okay! God has promised us no more than we can bear; and after the year we've had, I can't bear any more!

I had prayed many times through my pregnancy that God would protect the development of our child because emotionally I knew I had given it a poor start. The faith of my childhood made this prayer a natural one. My family had raised me to believe in the God who cares about the things that concern us.

The labor continued, and we found ourselves in the delivery room. Things were going much too slowly. The baby wasn't crowning, and the local anesthetic failed to ease the pain. Finally, we asked, "Is something wrong?"

Dr. Fuller replied, "I think your child is hydrocephalic."

Jerry asked, "What's that?"

Dr. Fuller hedged. "It's not good—"

And I screamed, "It's water on the brain!"

Realizing then that he couldn't ease us into the news, Dr. Fuller continued, "And if it's born alive, it probably won't live long."

Just moments earlier, I had refused sedation. I now began screaming, "Put me out! Put me out!" This time the doctor refused. He could not proceed without a second medical opinion.

2

The God Who Cares

Shall I look to the mountain gods for help? No! My help is from Jehovah who made the mountains! And the heavens too! (Ps. 121:1-2, TLB).

The delivery room came alive! The nurses began naming doctors who were scheduled to be there, and Dr. Fuller responded, "No," to each doctor they named. He began pacing the floor, then instinctively walked to the delivery room door, looked out, and shouted, "There's Dr. Brown! Come here!" And Dr. Brown strode into the delivery room.

I was still shouting, "Put me out!" when Jerry shouted, "Honey, that's Julia's husband! Aren't you Julia's husband?" They got acquainted while Dr. Brown scrubbed up, confirmed the diagnosis, escorted Jerry out of the room, and consoled him. Meanwhile, I continued to shout, "Put me out!" and an anesthetist "just happened" to be walking by my door. But . . .

Julia was my Bible Study Fellowship leader whom I adored. She had shared with us how her husband's life had changed since he had started praying each morning before leaving for work—and that morning he "just happened" to be walking by my door after that prayer! Few people in Bible Study Fellowship knew Julia's husband was an obstetrician. Employment is not discussed in the Bible study. She had picked me up one morning when my car wasn't working, so in conversation I had asked. I could remember griping to God about my car being broken down and saying, "If You want me in that Bible study, the least You can do is keep my car running!" Now I was really eating those words! Even seven months earlier, God had been at work preparing me for what was to come and readying those He was to use to help me. With a common name like Brown we wouldn't have made the connection without the prior knowledge.

The anesthetist was finally ready, and, in spite of my cries for sedation, I fought it with all my might! In the form of Dr. Brown, God himself had walked in to say, "I'm in control. I can handle what's happening. You and I together will make it." Not once did God give me false hope, promising the baby would be okay, but He said, "We'll make it! I'm bigger than what's happening, and you belong to Me." Just before I went under, I felt a deep sense of God's power. I knew He was there, guiding the doctors and caring for me.

I became aware again that my body was tense—I came back fighting, just as I had gone out. As I began to awaken from the anesthetic, I heard the voices of my loved ones speaking to me. My grandmother who had raised me was quoting her favorite poem: "God hath not promised skies always blue . . . But God hath promised strength for the day." This was not just something going through my mind—I heard the actual voice of Gram, as she had said it so often, with the inflections in her voice emphasizing she had found it to be true. With the same conviction in his voice, I heard Jerry's dad say to me, "My mommy always told me [then, in Grandmommy's precious voice], 'Sonny, His grace is sufficient!'" I heard Margie, my special aunt and "Mom," reminding me, as she did so often, "Just remember, ALL things work together for good."

How very important it is that we build up a foundation of faith in our children! I have thought it strange that it was the voices of those I love on earth that I heard instead of the voice of Jesus—or a favorite Bible verse—coming to me. But that is really the way God has planned life, isn't it? He uses human people to convey His message. He uses human parents to build faith into their children. He had given me a rich heritage, so it was only natural that I would draw from it in my time of need to find strength. I'm so thankful those I love built into me faith rather than bitterness. God impressed upon my heart the reality of the statements I had just heard and reminded me that I could face my problems knowing that God was in charge.

My muscles continued to spasm, and I became aware of the nurses' voices. I heard one nurse say, "She's tense," and felt them check my vitals. I realized they were watching me very closely, but I could not speak or respond even though I could hear what was going on.

Finally, I found the strength to ask, "Is my baby alive?" It's strange that would be my first question, because I had already begun to detach myself from my child. Before going under, I had been thinking, We never wanted an only child, but it will be okay. I'm so thankful God has given us Jeff. Life is such a miracle! I'm so thankful Jeff is healthy. I don't mean to minimize those words—they're true (more so today than they were back then). But in the midst of my tragedy, God gave me a thankful heart rather than allowing me to dwell on the negative. In my heart I was trying to let go of the child I had carried and loved for nine months—and I couldn't do that. I had to know, and I had to hope.

The nurses told me the baby had been "born alive" and that it was a boy. They then sent for the doctor, avoiding any further questions. I was so surprised to have a boy. The pregnancy had been so different from my first one; in my mind, this child had the temperament of a tender, wiggly little girl.

As kindly as he could, the doctor gave me the medical

details of the delivery. He encouraged me that there *might* be hope for Justin. He had drained 1½ cups of fluid from his head to allow for a vaginal delivery. My mind heard what he was saying, but I couldn't bring myself to ask a question or respond at all. Deep inside I knew that there was little hope for our child—but deep inside, I also knew that with God all things are possible.

I called for Jerry, and the nurses rushed to find him. During the few minutes that lapsed, my mind went to work again. Under the sedative, thoughts rushed in that I had no power to control or shut out. In contrast to my thoughts of deep, godly power, the negative set in: "There is a price for sin. Had Jerry's drinking caused this? Were we paying for our sins by sacrificing the life of the son we had created?"

Before I had time to dwell on these tormenting, legalistic thoughts, God replaced them. I heard the familiar voices of Dave and Orville, our ministers, talking to Jerry. We were so new to their flock that I was literally overwhelmed with gratitude that they had come to comfort Jerry, who hadn't had the benefit of a sedative as I had. They visited briefly, prayed with me, and left.

In our first moment alone, Jerry grabbed me and said, "After all I've put you through, I'm *so* sorry you have to face this! I deserve it, but you don't." All was forgiven! God filled my soul with a deep gratitude that we had each other. There was no resentment that we were going to face tough times.

3

Peace Through Recycled Prayer

The peace of God, which surpasses human under-
standing, will keep constant guard over your hearts
and minds as they rest in Christ Jesus (Phil. 4:7, Phillips).

Within seconds, the phone rang! My Uncle Bob, who is a
minister, said, "I want to tell you three things: 1. Don't try to
understand what has happened; humanly, that is impossible.
2. Don't blame yourselves or each other for what has
happened—there is no blame for handicap, and you can't
live with that load of guilt. Use this to love each other more;
don't allow it to draw you apart. 3. Above all, *don't blame God!*
He does not send things like this! He allows them to happen
because we live in a world that is imperfect because sin
reigns, but *He does not cause them!* He can teach us through
them, and He can bring good from them, but *He does not send*
them." In closing, he added, "Oh, I guess, humanly speaking,
you'll have to ask, 'Why?' but when you do, remember that
you won't get an answer."

What peace filled me! I was *totally released* at that moment from the torment of guilt and the burden of *blame!* My
legalistic accusations were a thing of the past. I didn't have to
know why, in a spiritual sense, or who had caused it. I only
had to know that God could bring me through it. From that
moment, and on into the months that followed. My "whys"
were answered with the "peace that passeth understanding."

God lifted us out of the world we had lived in and placed us in a new world—one walled by His grace. God made us radiant in the midst of our struggle and our hurt. What stabbed us from the outside was met with a wall of *joy, peace, confidence in God.* I had seen in others the "peace of God, which passeth all understanding." Now I was experiencing it firsthand. As we had watched Phyllis, Jerry's mother, struggle with cancer, we had become discouraged—but she never had. She was radiant! She would encourage us and build our faith! She never appeared to feel discouragement, even though she sometimes suffered almost unbearably. She had a peace. Now that peace was ours.

God sometimes lifts us right out of our situation and gives a radiant, glowing peace and faith that we don't deserve. At other times, He appears to hide His face from us and seem oblivious to our tears, even though we cry that we don't deserve our fate. Since Justin's death (almost two years now), I have lived on the dark side of God's love; but I believe that the same God that appeared to me over and over again during Justin's lifetime is still caring for me, loving me and "working together" for me now, even though I cannot see Him! We must open up our lives to receive the peace of God, but it is God himself who must give what we need. He responds when we need Him—and the peace never comes ahead of time. Sometimes, during our hour of need, we can't feel that peace. Yet God knows our needs far better than we do, and He will send the peace when His timing matches our readiness.

The peace that God gave us was not just for a moment. Justin lived 4½ months; and daily during those months, God walked with us, giving peace. There were hurts and frustrations—but there was *always* that deep, settled peace and knowledge that God was in control. I began to know a little of what the Garden of Eden must have been like when

Adam walked and talked with God daily. I would call; immediately I would be aware of His presence ministering to me. I don't claim to understand the power of prayer, but I believe in it more than I used to. Jerry described our experience best. He believed that it was a direct result of prayer that we were so blessed.

In Jerry's words, "People from all over the world were praying for us! Some friends, relatives, prayer groups that they belonged to—and even people that we hadn't heard from for years—were moved to pray for us, in some cases not even knowing why. God received these little 'rays' from all over the world and recycled them through a magnifying glass onto us. The power of these prayers mushroomed beneath us and literally lifted us above the world and its limited vision."

It is hard for me to speak of God's goodness and peace during our tough times without feeling under a terrible burden to live on that level of victory at all times! We *all* prefer the mountaintop to the valleys in our lives. We begin to expect the spectacular with God to be His normal way of dealing with us. Then, when things return to normal and His power is no longer needed in such large amounts, we are loaded with guilt and depression because we miss it; or when we fail or sin, we are afraid to admit it for fear of letting someone down, so we bury our thoughts and become hypocritical. The devil jumps right in to say to us, "Look at your faith—you're something special! God must really admire you! You've got it made!" Then, inevitably, because our pride takes over, the devil adds, "You blew it—better not let anyone know or you'll let God down!"And here comes the hypocrite!

What terrible pressure I lived under during these beautiful days, crying to all who would listen, "No! I'm normal! I'm even weak! God is the One who is my power! I couldn't have this attitude myself—it's God speaking through me." It's so important to me that people understand this. God gives to *anyone* who has a need and calls on His name. He doesn't give just a "positive" attitude—He gives a total peace!

That peace doesn't make any sense at all. We should have been complaining, but we just couldn't do it. God filled our lives with *peace* that didn't need an explanation. Our baby was hopelessly handicapped. But it was *okay!* The medical bills were going to be high. But it was *okay!* The doctors gave hopeless reports. But it was *okay!* The decisions had to be made—and they all hurt—but it was *okay!* Even when the decisions were made, we couldn't let go. But it was *okay!*

I don't know of any other way to say it. We knew we faced a hopeless situation. People cried for us, and we encouraged them. We couldn't do this in our own power, but God became our Strength and our Peace. In spite of the negative reports, we just couldn't be quiet. God was in control, and He is good, and it would all be *okay!* I even tried to keep my mouth shut—but I couldn't. I just had to tell everyone I talked to that God was taking care of me, and everything would be *okay!*

4

Loving! How It Hurts!

"My power shows up best in weak people" (2 Cor. 12:9, TLB).

They wheeled me to my room, and I saw a yellow bedspread. I'll never forget the pain. I thought, He died! I knew it would be "best," but *when you hurt, "best" doesn't really matter.* The child I had loved and carried for nine months already was a life—a personality. A tender creature who needed to be cuddled and nurtured. When you have a boy, you get a blue bedspread; when you have a girl, you get a pink bedspread. Mine was an ugly yellow!

It was some time before I could bring myself to ask, for fear of the answer. Finally I asked, and Jerry replied, "I've seen him! He looks perfect! You'd never know anything was wrong. He's still alive." I was so relieved—yet so apprehensive. Jerry wanted us to hear from the doctors and decide what to do before I had the chance to see him—and, although I had mixed emotions, I didn't argue. To see was to risk loving more and hurting more. I didn't have the energy to see him. In looking back, I realize that I was trying to detach myself. I didn't want to see him if I couldn't have him, but neither could I let him go.

Jerry called our boy by his name—Justin David. We had selected that name, but I had had reservations. Now it seemed so perfect—Justin, meaning "the Just"; David, meaning "God's anointed." Even the name we had chosen became

23

a comfort to me. This child, after all, belonged to God! He wouldn't live long. He really seemed like God's chosen one. I had worried that "the Just" would be a hard name to live up to—he wouldn't have to. The name belonged to him.

As I look back now, the things that comforted me seem so strange. God filled my heart and opened my eyes to see things from a different perspective. Rather than being resentful that God would take my child to heaven, I found true comfort in knowing that when he got there, he would have a "Gammy" waiting to care for him; she always favored the "little" ones.

We couldn't wait for the doctors. Jerry suggested that we go look at Justin, encouraging me to love him regardless of the outlook. How guilty I would feel today if I had refused to love my own baby! God loves us in spite of our imperfections, but we try to dish out our love only to those most deserving of it. I tried to keep from really loving my own child because I didn't want to hurt any more. I knew, as things were then, that if I chose to love more, I would hurt more.

As we walked to the intensive care nursery, I began to tell myself that we were just looking at "a" baby. This was some little "stranger"; this was a child I didn't yet know. I felt that way when Jeff was born. I had to learn how to be a mother! I was so overwhelmed with my new role in life that I had to keep telling myself over and over again that he was really mine and that I was really his. I thought that Justin could be a "little stranger"; that I could detach myself. As I neared the window, I was in a state of total shock. I could have picked him out of 5,000 babies! The reality that this was "my" child stabbed me! He looked like my baby pictures— and he looked like Jeff's baby pictures—and *he belonged to me!* I realized, then, that he was my baby, and that I would claim him and love him deeply regardless of his physical or mental handicap, even though it meant losing somewhere down the line. He looked so perfect. He was so beautiful. It was hard to believe that something could be so wrong! The agony of what to do became so great—but, from that moment on, we knew we loved him!

I still had so much to learn, though.

5

Handicap
Seen Through New Eyes

As thy days, so shall thy strength be (Deut. 33:25).

Dr. Weinberg, our pediatrician, came without delay, but the news was not good. He told us Justin would be a vegetable all his life. He might live one day; he might live 40 years. There was shunt surgery available—but he didnt recommend it in "hopeless" cases, for fear of prolonging life. Justin's head was severely damaged from the blockage—probably he had no brain tissue left at all. The blockage happened very early in pregnancy—during the first three months at least, perhaps during the first three weeks. The brain had no chance at all to develop. I said, "But he looks so perfect!" The doctor's words followed: "From the ears down, you have a perfect, healthy, beautiful, normal baby! But . . . "

Hydrocephalus means "water on the brain." This happens because the normal opening between the head and the spinal column, for some unknown reason, closes. The fluid that flows from the brain through the spinal column is then trapped inside the brain. The head enlarges to accommodate the fluid; the brain is "squeezed" to allow for it. When doctors measure a baby's head, as a routine part of every "well baby" check, they are watching for this abnormal growth. Hydrocephalus can occur for many reasons and at any stage in development; the prognosis of the case depends upon when it happened, why it happened, and how much damage has been done prior to its being treated. Justin was considered hopeless because his blockage occurred so early in his development and progressed for so long without treatment. In his case, it couldn't have been discovered before the seventh month of pregnancy which would already have been too late. Normally, when this happens, the fetus will abort. Sometimes it goes to full term; sometimes life goes on this way for 40 years.

Dr. Weinberg continued to tell us that Justin's head would grow to an enormous proportion—perhaps as large as his crib—and his body would hardly grow at all. Although he appeared normal at birth, daily his handicap would become more apparent.

Dr. Weinberg had been our pediatrician for three years. During this time, I had learned to respect him and trust his judgment. If he had a tendency to "stretch" the diagnosis, it was in the opposite direction of what he was saying. Never once had he alarmed me when I had taken Jeff in for a checkup. Usually, when I was upset, he would tease me until I relaxed; then he would examine and treat Jeff, calmly explaining his symptoms after I was in a relaxed frame of mind. If a specialist was needed, Dr. Weinberg would recommend "the best." He was never in a hurry, though, to call for surgery or specialist. The words I was hearing now, I knew, were true. He continued that we could elect to:

1. Shunt and do everything possible to save the life of our baby—in which case we would have to find a new pediatrician because, in his mind, this would be unethical.

2. Leave our baby as he is: treat any illness as it comes along.

27

3. Leave him as he is; make no effort to prolong life
    if he contracts an illness. Love and care for
    him while we have him.

I said, "But I don't care *what* he is! I can't let him suffer!"

The doctor replied, firmly, but kindly, "He won't suffer.
He doesn't have the brain capacity to feel pain."

He then told us we had three more choices—decisions—
to make. We could:

1. Institutionalize him.
2. Take him home and love and care for him for as
    long as that is physically possible.
3. Place him in a home equipped to care for hand-
    icapped children, nearby, where he would
    be with other children with similar disabil-
    ities and where we could visit.

Handicapped!
    Brain damaged!
        Mentally retarded!
            Deformed!
                Birth defect!
                    Institution!
                        Enormous head size!

What a nightmare of words! What a blow! Those awful
words rang in my ears and haunted me as I tried to sleep.

Before leaving, the doctor reminded us that we must
consider *all* members of the family in making our decisions—
and all aspects of our ability, including financial. He reminded us that Justin was not "sick" and could not stay in the
hospital; he was deformed. He had already contacted one of
the finest neurosurgeons in California to verify his findings
and we should wait for a final decision until we heard from
him. There was a possibility that he would uncover something new—something that Dr. Weinberg had overlooked.

In my heart, I knew that the words I had just heard would be confirmed. I had complete confidence in his medical opinion—and I appreciated his kindness and tenderness as he talked to us. More than anything, though, I appreciated his having the integrity to tell us the truth. *It hurts far more to be the victim of a kindness cover-up than to hear the hurtful truth.* To hang on to hope when there is none would be far more frustrating than to deal with hopelessness.

Visitors began to "sneak" in to see us—and the hospital personnel beautifully "looked the other way." I found the hospital staff to be so warm and loving in the midst of our tragedy. They broke every "rule" they possibly could to accommodate our wishes and ease our pain. Our friends immediately began to respond to our hurt with phone calls and notes of encouragement. My heart reached out and touched theirs as they groped for words. Several years before, I had been in their shoes. My college roommate's first baby had been hydrocephalic, stillborn—and I had to comfort her. Words were just so inadequate, and I felt helpless to ease her pain. As I looked back, I realized that it was she who eased my pain; now it was my turn. God gave me peace and power to respond to what I heard, and the calls of my friends warmed my heart and spoke to me of His love. Someone in the midst of tragedy needs your person, not your words.

Those who gave advice were truly messengers from God—the advice came at my hour of need and rang true in my heart. Most, however, simply said, "I'm sorry," reaffirming their love and support. I desperately needed that, even more than I needed the best advice available.

God always insists on total honesty. We believed and accepted Justin's condition; we didn't argue that it couldn't be true, thus deceiving ourselves. We turned over the bitter truth to a God who is greater than our minds can comprehend. He made that bitter truth bearable—even beautiful—when we opened up our lives to receive His goodness.

We asked if we could see and hold Justin in our room. Isn't it strange how we shy away from a handicap! Just hours earlier we had discussed "rooming in" and having him beside us: now I was really surprised that I could even hold him. I thought of him as "diseased." I wasn't sure I wanted to hold him. Thankfully, Jerry was!

The nurse brought him to us—sparkling clean and wrapped tightly in a blue blanket. She hugged him; then, as she handed him to us, she said, "This is a heaven baby! Love him while you have him. He's so precious!" From then on he was spoken of as "our heaven baby." What a difference! No longer did we think of him as "handicapped," "brain damaged," "mentally retarded," or "hydrocephalic." We thought of him as a "heaven baby," loaned to us for a while to love. I still had a lot to learn about loving at the risk of hurting, but this beautiful nurse had opened a doorway to me!

We had a roomful of people and the hospital let us hold our baby—unheard of with hospital policy—but someone knew I needed the support of family when I saw Justin for the first time. They helped me to see that he was indeed a beautiful baby, easy to love. There was no reason to cry and dwell in self-pity. Like any mother when she sees her child for the first time, I immediately unwrapped him "to see if he was all there." We looked upon the body of a perfect, beautiful, healthy baby.

What a surge of mixed emotions! How could someone so perfect and beautiful on the outside be so hopelessly handicapped? I guess even this has its spiritual parallel. The outside never really shows what is on the inside. Most important, though, is that all—sick and well, rich and poor, good and bad—are objects of God's unchanging love.

Word came from the neurosurgeon—almost like a tape

recording of Dr. Weinberg's earlier message: "Vegetable . . . brain damaged . . . hopeless." Dr. Bonner was kind to answer our questions, willing to spare whatever time we needed to help us. He assured us this shouldn't happen again if we someday had another child. The verdict on Justin was the same: Hopeless! Now, though, the message came to parents who had seen, held, and loved their child. Each time, the pain went a little deeper.

What torture we lived in for a few hours! It was bearable only because God gave us thoughtful friends who called every once in a while to say, "We care. We will support your decision, whatever it is."

Decisions of any kind have always been a burden to me. So many questions raced through my mind!

What would a handicapped child do to our home?

How would it affect our precious Jeff?

How would it affect our own relationship?

Could I, personally, care for a handicapped child?

Did I have any right to think of myself at a time like this?

Would I abuse a handicapped child? Would I, subconsciously, decide he would be better off in heaven and try to "help God out a little" by neglecting or undernourishing him? These are brutal thoughts—yet they are true! I am insecure caring for a normal baby, let alone an abnormal one.

Would I hurt every time I touched or looked at him, realizing he was dying?

Would I go to the other extreme and overprotect Justin?

Would I neglect Jeff trying to care for Justin?

What was our moral obligation to Justin?

What was our moral obligation to Jeff?

Was there a difference in our obligation, as parents, to a very normal child as compared to a child who would be a vegetable all his life?

Could we, morally, let an institution care for a child we had created?

Could we do this spiritually?

Knowing that the stress and strain of a handicapped child would surely affect Jeff, would we be doing what was right for him to try to care for Justin in our home?

Would it be worse on Jeff to think that we could give up the child we had been planning for over the past nine months—the little brother or sister he had watched grow in "Mommy's tummy"?

How would we explain to Jeff that we had come to the hospital to get our baby, but the baby was very sick and we couldn't bring him home? Our close friends were shortly to bring home their new baby, too.

How could we explain handicap to a child? Could he understand that our baby wasn't normal and would never be able to run and play with him like his friend's brothers and sisters did?

What is the *right* thing to do? This question haunted me! I had always tried to do what was "right"; but nothing in this situation was. At best, we could choose the lesser of two evils—and, with our limited knowledge, we didn't even know what that was!

What is right? What is right? What is right?

In spite of the nightmare I'm describing—and it was very real—I had within me an abnormal power—a deep confidence that God was bigger than our situation. I found strength to make this decision, with none to spare; then I could rest for the next big struggle we were to face. My strength *never* came a day before I needed it—but it was *always* there at our hour of decision. At just the right moment, the phone would ring, or the mailman would bring a package with a book that contained our message from God, or a song would be played on the radio or race through my

32

mind with a message that God was in control, or a doctor would say the words that spoke to my heart. I had an uncanny sense during Justin's life of God's timing. Somehow, I almost knew what would happen before it did.

God's promises are true—as your days come, you will find your strength to be equal to them. He has not promised us strength *before* we need it. He has not promised us more strength than we need. But He has promised us that in our hour of need, *His strength will be there! And it always is!* Even when we cannot see or feel it, we must *know* that it is there because God has promised it—and God is a God of integrity. He cannot break His promise.

This time, God sent His peace and strength through a well-timed phone call.

6

Decisions, Decisions, Decisions

There is therefore now no condemnation to them which are in Christ Jesus (Rom. 8:1).

Guilt overwhelmed me as I looked at our choices. I would decide to bring Justin home—then I would send myself into a guilt trip about caring for Jeff! Then I would decide to try to place Justin in a home—I couldn't even *say* the word *institutionalize!*—but guilt would overpower me at the thought of asking someone else to care for a life that I had created. Jerry shared these feelings and passed them on to our friends in his "nightly reports."

My doctor released me from the hospital but told me I could not go home unless Justin could stay—he wanted me to have complete rest. We were faced with an immediate decision: Should I go home? Home has never sounded so beautiful! We were agonizing, feeling the pressure of deciding, when the phone rang. One of my good friends and fellow teachers called to say:

"Jerry told me you were having trouble making your decisions. I know you are a Christian, so I want to share some verses with you." Charlienne then quoted most of Romans 8 to me—the familiar verses I had heard so many times. By the time she finished speaking, I felt that I had never ever heard them before, as God gave them a new meaning in my heart. There is *no condemnation* to those who are in Christ. If we are to share in His glory, we must also share in His suffering. *"All things work together for good."*

Then she added, "When we're God's children, *it doesn't matter what decision we make!* He has promised us that He won't condemn us! He has promised us that *all* things will work together for good. Whatever decision we make, somewhere down the line it will be good. Even if it's the *wrong* decision, and we have honestly turned the situation over to Him, somewhere down the line, He will reverse it for us or block it. It will all work together for good! Even if our decision seems selfish, when we commit it to God in complete confidence, He overrules."

What freedom! I had *never* known that side of God's love! I had turned my life over to God at age five—and God had been good to me. But I had been a true legalist. I had always labored under the burden of making the "right" decision for God—of doing what was "right"—trusting my human judgment! Now, when I was faced with *all* wrong, terribly wrong choices, my humanity and legalism failed me! It was in that failure that the love of God could take over. And it did. Never before nor since have I been so free. So loved! So cared for! I could have complete confidence in God. I can't change things or make good come from them, but I know the God who can. And God will. And God did!

We hung up the phone and prayed: "God, help us to remember that Justin belongs to You. We had dedicated him to You before he was even conceived. Let us not forget that You have known him much better than we have, and let us not forget that our children are not really ours. We take our hands off of him now and turn his life over to You! You haven't promised us that all things are good—this is not good. But You have promised us that good can come from all things. This handicap is not from You, the Author of all goodness. But You are bigger and more powerful than any handicap—and You are bigger and more powerful than the evil one who sends handicap into our world. You have promised this will work together for good. Even though we can see nothing good coming from it in the future, we turn Justin's life over to You and ask You to shine Your love through it—and through this helpless, hopeless little body, bring good into the world. Help us to make the best decision—and take the decision we make and reverse it if we err—and don't ever let us forget that our children are Yours, just loaned to us to love—and that we belong to You—and that with You, all things are possible! In Jesus' name. Amen."

When I realize how totally and directly God answered that prayer over the next few months, I am still amazed. Many times we had to remind ourselves of Prov. 3:5-6, especially "lean not unto thine own understanding," for nothing that happened made sense, humanly speaking.

I could remember thinking before Justin was born that he had to be okay because I had had all I could bear. I could now say within me, "I can't bear it—so God filled my being and bore it for me." I now see God's promise that we won't have more than we can bear, *not* as a promise that things will be easy for us, but as a promise that when we come to the end of our strength, our hope, our stamina, our fears—He will *still be beside us—and He will become* our Hope, our Strength, our Perseverance, our *Joy*. I believe this because God has promised it. Dynamically, it was true during Justin's lifetime; I cannot see it going through dark times, but I believe that someday I will be able, in retrospect, to proclaim that God was *still* my Strength, even when I could not see, feel, or hear Him in the midst of my depression! Even though all I can see are shattered pieces, He will still "work together" for my good.

The hospital social worker told us of the Central Valley Regional Center. We decided to place Justin through this organization. This is a step between the home and an institution. The homes care for a maximum of six handicapped children with similar disabilities and of similar ages. We would maintain legal custody and have visiting rights. And God located a home just a few miles from our own! Crippled Children's organization underwrites most of the expenses when there is a financial need, and the homes are staffed with people trained to work with the handicapped. In addition, therapists visit the homes on a regular basis to help the children develop to their maximum capacity.

I felt a little like a freeloader, but the social worker reassured me: "You've been paying for this for years through your state taxes. Just be thankful that your taxes are going for such a good cause." I must admit that I don't complain about taxes as much as I used to. I am so thankful to live in a country that values a human life, regardless of its potential. I was proud that my taxes had, in the past, helped another child—even without my knowledge.

Our decision was both selfish and logical. I knew I could not provide the care that Justin would receive there. Emotionally, too, at that time, I could not bear to watch my baby die. I had such a fear of death and of how I would respond to it. I look on death so differently now. I think that now I could love Justin and be thankful that I had him, one day at a time. At that time, though, I couldn't face it. Neither could I face an institution; so the Regional Center—in principle, similar to a rest home for the elderly—was a compromise.

We prayed, very simply, that God would reverse our decision if it was wrong. I think we really hoped somehow He would. Again we claimed His promise that all things work together for good. We prayed, too, that God would take Justin to heaven soon—that he wouldn't have to live to be a 40-year-old vegetable.

We realized that God could choose to heal Justin, but, at

the time I didn't think He would. Deep inside, we never lost sight of the promise that "With God all things are possible"; but deep inside, I felt that God would bring good in some way other than total healing in a physical sense. Perhaps I was afraid to claim healing because if God should take him to heaven, I would hurt again. Perhaps I was afraid to claim healing for fear of what I would say if the healing wasn't complete. Perhaps I felt unworthy of healing. Perhaps I was afraid of what such a miracle would do to a child with a free will. At any rate, my confidence was in God's power to handle the situation as it was—not based on the miracle of physical healing—although I never lost sight of the fact that physical healing was possible. Somehow, too, I knew that Justin was not going to die, even though through our human eyes, that seemed best.

7

Home Without Justin

Fix your thoughts on what is true and good and right.
Think about things that are pure and lovely, and dwell
on the fine, good things in others. Think about all you
can praise God for and be glad about (Phil. 4:8, TLB).

How do you describe the agony of going home from the hospital without your baby? Of looking through the nursery window as you leave at the tiny, helpless, beautiful life that you wish was going with you? Of realizing that this might be the last time you see that child alive? It would be agonizing to leave without your child even when the outlook was good. Multiply the blackness, the hopelessness, the helplessness, the despair—and you have a glimpse of what it's like to leave your baby, knowing you'll never have him—someone else will care for him . . . He'd be better off dead—and wishing you could erase the past nine months from your memory, calling it a bad nightmare. The love of our friends helped to make it bearable, but the blackness was very real.

Just a few months before Justin was born, I had watched *The Hiding Place.* I remembered hearing that there was no hole so deep, no sin so ugly, no persecution so painful that the love of God could not reach it. I had gone home and cried, "God, I've served You all my life—yet I don't have that kind of faith. I couldn't go through persecution like they did." It began to dawn on me that God hadn't asked me to go through persecution, so I didn't need that kind of faith. Leaving Justin was a part of my "suffering" for Christ—and *His love went deeper than the hurt.* The pain does not go away, as we would like to believe it does, but *the love of God goes deeper.* We bear the hurt; we reach our end of endurance; we think we can bear no more; but the love of God is still there, ministering to our spirits and giving us strength to hold on. We need only open our hearts to receive.

Jerry and I made several other decisions at this time. I don't think I would have had the faith or insight to make them alone, but they were the key to God's work in our lives over the next several months. We remembered Dr. Finch, one of our dear minister friends, saying that it doesn't matter what our circumstances are in life—we cannot control them; what matters is our attitude toward those circumstances—we alone control that! We could allow ourselves to become isolated and bitter, or we could choose to become more loving, more outgoing, more positive people through our circumstances. We consciously decided that we would not allow this experience to embitter us and that we would allow God to work through us, making us better people because of our situation. We prayed to that end and asked God to give us insight, love, and a positive attitude. I do not believe it is possible to be positive in the midst of life's hurts without the touch of God! Positive thinking is great—but without the healing touch of God, it is hypocritical—it is, in a sense, living a lie. We prayed, then, for God's touch on our feelings and our attitudes. The choice was ours to make—and we made it. The work was God's to do—and He did it.

We didn't stop there—we realized that it would be hard for our friends and relatives to reach out to us. The hardest friends with whom to share the good news that I was pregnant were the ones who had been trying unsuccessfully for five years themselves. The hesitancy was ours, granted; yet no one could have been more joyous for us than they. But now we realized that others would feel hesitant to share their "normal" babies with us—so we went to them, requesting that they allow us to love their children, and that they call on us to baby-sit occasionally. And we assured them that we would respond out of love, not out of jealousy.

You see, we had another choice. We could reach out and love other children and babies and become more loving, more Christlike people; or we could isolate ourselves, have a "pity party," and become more bitter, lonely people. That's not much of a choice, granted, but it's a lot easier to run from your hurts than it is to face them. Most people choose bitterness just because they can't bear to face up to their pain.

It's "normal" to be jealous of others who have what you want, so this was another area that we had to take to God in prayer. God can heal that jealousy; we can't. We can "decide" that we will not be jealous—but without the healing touch of God, we cannot unselfishly love others who are more fortunate than we. God has healed that jealousy in my life. Yes, I miss my baby. Yes, I hurt. Yes, sometimes when I hold another baby, I go home and cry. Yes, sometimes I don't wait to go home to cry; I sit and cry while I hold and love another child—and it's been two years! But *I do not wish that were my child or wish that someone else had to hurt with me or for me!* God has healed that!

I think this is really important. God does not take away the pain; He gives us a positive attitude and love toward others who have what we don't. This was a hard lesson for me to learn—I thought that as a Christian, I wouldn't hurt anymore when I had given something to God. Not true. But God's love goes deeper than my hurt and makes it bearable. It "works together" for good. We must make the choice, when there is one so clear-cut as this; then we must give the work to God to do. We do not have the power to do the work, but we belong to the one God who does!

This attitude choice is not a one-time thing. We can, consciously or subconsciously, reverse that decision at any time. God does not take away our free will because we have chosen to serve Him. Sometimes I really wish He would—life would be so much easier—but He doesn't. That means that when we catch ourselves being negative, responding out of pity or out of jealousy, we must again take it to God. I usually say something like: "Here I go again, God! I couldn't handle it then, and I can't handle it now! Heal my attitude and help me to love; take away the bitterness and resentment that I feel. I can be angry at what I see, but I will die if I become jealous and look inward. I can't look outward in my own power just now, so You do it for me. Make my attitude and outlook what You want it to be." I don't always feel different after I pray that prayer. I don't always let go of my jealousy at that time. But God *always* does His part, and when I reach the place where I am willing to let Him open my eyes, I can see through His wisdom. That brings true healing!

We made a sort of unconscious decision along with the conscious ones; we decided to open our lives up to other people. I don't think we were aware of that choice—and perhaps this was merely a result of our answered prayer. But God showered us with blessings from our friends. He opened our hearts to receive their love, and their love became a part of our strength during our hard times. I recognize this now because I have seen people, both Christian and non-Christian, go through tough times and refuse the love of others, thereby isolating themselves. We wouldn't have made it without our friends. *I don't remember even one lonely evening during Justin's lifetime.* When we needed love, the phone would ring; the mailman would bring a note that said, in some way, "I care"; the doorbell would ring—our friends stood by our sides. They allowed us the freedom to hurt, and God loved us through their acceptance.

I didn't realize just how much our friends were a gift from God until several months later. I heard a speaker describe the lonely hours she spent holding her child until he died; her friends were nonexistent; they didn't know what to say to her, how to comfort her, how to face hopeless handicap. They just sort of dropped her and went their own ways. Immediately I began to realize that fellowship is one of the sweetest benefits of being a Christian and going through tough times. Christian friends don't know what to say either—but they know the One who does! Christian friends feel awkward under the circumstances, too—but they know the One who feels comfortable. Our friends really ministered to us. They didn't know what to say or how to comfort either—but they were there. They stood by us—we went out to eat together; we visited in each other's homes; sometimes we ignored our tragedy and spent a much-needed night out. Sometimes we were so burdened we had to speak—they listened without condemnation and assured us they cared. They couldn't give us advice—even the best-trained doctors couldn't do that. But they could listen, let us know they cared, and pray for us—and they did!

God richly and tenderly cares for His children through His gift of Christian fellowship. My speaker friend found Christ through her lonely experience; I was so much more fortunate. I knew Christ *before* my tragedy; it hurt, but it was never lonely because He cared for me through my friends.

It is important that we understand that God is no respecter of persons. Somehow we have the mistaken idea that if we are truly serving Christ as we should, our lives will be rosy. Tragedy may strike, but we will live above that tragedy and praise God and cease to hurt because we belong to God. I used to think I had backslidden if I questioned God's wisdom or if I bore some pain. I believe now that life is full of hurts. It doesn't matter whether you're a Christian or not.

Somewhere along the line you'll hurt deeply! The test of your faith is whether or not you can trust God *while* you are hurting and praise Him for being God even when you don't understand why He'd allow a bad thing to happen. The true test is if you can really believe that He is in control when you disagree with the wisdom of what you see happening. I sometimes say, "God, I sure wouldn't have done it that way if I had been You!" But, when I'm really honest, I must also say, in retrospect, "God, You really *did* do it the right way, didn't You!" If, in retrospect, I can say that, faith must also say, before the fact, "God, I believe in Your integrity; I can't see where good will come, but I believe it will because I believe in a good God who *always* keeps His promises!"

We prayed, as we bore our sorrow, that God would give us a positive attitude about what we were to face—that He would allow us to see through His eyes. I am still amazed that He answered that prayer!

8

Tough Questions on Compassion

Don't criticize, and then you won't be criticized (Matt. 7:1, TLB).

Justin was allowed to stay in the hospital for the week-end after I was released. I felt as I left the hospital that I couldn't bear to see him anymore; I tried to walk out and begin forgetting the events of the past few days. I thought of my responsibility to Jeff and how much he needed me now (really, how much *I* needed *him!*). I really intended to walk out and leave my baby.

Jerry, though, had other plans. That evening while I was safe at home with relatives and friends who had come to care for us, Jerry returned to the hospital to spend some time with his son. The next day, Jerry insisted that I, too, return to the hospital to spend some time with Justin. Without his encouragement, I don't think I would have done it—I would have run away! I offered excuses; "We'll,have to get another baby-sitter for Jeff. He needs me." But Jerry was insistent. He arranged for the baby-sitter and took me back to the hospital.

We learned the routine in the nursery—scrub up, put on your hospital garb, take off all jewelry, etc.; then you can hold your child. They had a semiprivate viewing room in the intermediate care nursery where we could feed and rock Justin. Justin couldn't eat. We had to "pump" the nipple to get any food down him; even this process was slow, and it took him a long time to eat. He didn't know how to suck—the most basic of all responses. When hungry, he didn't cry. When uncomfortable for some reason, he might whimper. He never moved on his own; his eyes appeared to see nothing. I couldn't help remembering those bright, beautiful eyes I had seen the last time I held my baby in the hospital. Jeff had given me a good "looking over" when he was just hours old. As I remembered those bright expressive eyes that have always been Jeff's dominant feature, I began to realize how right the doctors were that Justin was hopelessly brain damaged.

In spite of all this, I couldn't help but be drawn to Justin in love. It didn't matter what the outlook, there was love in my child, and I had to respond to it. While we were holding him there, a "new" father came to see his baby. We started to move out of the room so he could come in—"hospital regulations." As we started to move, he said, "No, don't. I just want to know if it's a boy. I don't want to see it—just so it's a boy. Nothing else matters." The nurse proudly held his new son to the window; he quickly glanced at him, then left without another comment, motioning to her that he didn't care.

Can you imagine our emotions? How irate we were to see his stupidity! We wanted a healthy child—it didn't matter what—and our child was a hopeless case. While we were trying to cope with our situation, learning how to love in the midst of tragedy, this man had the audacity to say it doesn't matter what the baby looks like, whether he sees his child, whether he's okay or his wife is okay—just as long as it is a boy!

It didn't take God long to speak to us about our attitude, though. He simply said, "Judge not." The man's attitude is not our responsibility; ours is. If we allow ourselves to become judgmental of others, we will become filled with self-pity, self-righteousness, and bitterness. None of these emotions are healthy. We can be angry at what happens, but we must have compassion for a person with such a small capacity for love that he had to respond in that way. We can correct our shortcomings and be more thankful for each other by watching him. There are times when we have both the right and the responsibility to speak out against wrongdoings. Anger that is aimed at the wrong is healthy. Anger that is aimed at the inequity in life (we want a healthy child and don't have one, and he doesn't care and doesn't deserve a healthy child and probably won't love it anyway) is self-righteous self-pity. Such anger puts us in the judgment seat of God and says, "We are better." It also looks only at the small action that we see and makes a judgment out of ignorance. To do this is wrong—and God very beautifully healed my attitude toward other people during the days ahead.

It was so hard to leave Justin again. It wasn't quite as hard as the first separation—that blackness of going home without my baby—but it *just didn't quit hurting*. In the back of our minds and hearts at all times was the nagging reality that someone we had created and someone we were learning to love deeply whether or not we wanted to, was suffering. We prayed that God would take him to heaven soon. We prayed that Monday and a "substitute home" wouldn't have to come. And we hurt so deeply as we prayed that kind of a prayer. Deep inside, perhaps where we weren't even aware of it, we prayed that God would touch him—would perform a miracle. We wanted him whole, and we really didn't want him to go to heaven. We preferred that, though, to days or years of vegetation. We prayed at all times for God's will— and that, if it could be God's will, Justin would go to heaven rather than to another home. But Monday came . . .

And Monday had to be the blackest day that we could ever face! Justin was taken to the Sperling home by the social worker. At our request, we met them there and met Mrs.

47

Sperling, who was to be his foster mother. Oh, how I wanted to grab him out of the arms of that social worker and run! I think my entire body tried to launch out at this inequity. Yes, it had been my decision to place him—but the doctors had to be wrong. I wouldn't believe it. I would grab him and take him home and everything would be okay. Oh, there is agony in facing the truth! There is eternal torment in living a lie, but there is agony in facing reality!

Mrs. Sperling was a kind, grandmotherly lady. I walked into her home and saw statues—and smelled cigarette smoke. I thought, *My* son can't be raised here! Then I realized that *my* son wouldn't be *raised*—he would be cared for. He couldn't be trained to be a "moral" person. The challenges that would normally be present couldn't be an issue.

I don't know how others might feel in such a situation, but it *still* hurts me. I thought I had cried until I could cry no more, but the utterly helpless agony of placing your child into the care of someone else cannot be equaled! Even among your best friends and relatives, there are none who would do things exactly as you would like them done (you, yourself, don't always do what you feel is "right" for your children). Now my son was to be in the care of someone I didn't even know, and to cover up the hurt that I was facing, I launched out to criticize her. How did I ever make it? I remember that Jerry left for work from the Sperling home; my sister Velda and I drove to a nearby parking lot and cried . . . and cried . . . and cried.

God has promised us "strength for the day"; and somehow we made it. We had no strength to spare. We couldn't have faced anything else. But God did not promise us that we would finish our day with strength for tomorrow. I learned to depend on God's promises and try to face one day at a time.

As we visited Justin in his new home over the next few days, I began to make an effort to love the other children who were there. Handicap was a new world to me. I had heard about "institutions" and "handicap"; but my life had been sheltered. The handicaps of people I had known had been relatively minor. It was not normal for me to feel enough at ease around someone with a handicap to allow them to talk about it. I prayed for God's guidance. I realized how much it would mean to me if, when the other parents visited, they would reach out in love to *my* son, so I tried to do that with their children. I saw a little boy with bright, shining eyes full of love. He was an obvious favorite among the workers. When I asked what was wrong with him, I was told that the Sperlings were trying to adopt him—his mother never visited; she had tried to abort him by overdosing while she was pregnant. He was mentally normal, apparently, but would be a cripple with a kidney problem all his life as a result of this attempted abortion.

I was greeted one day by a rather large girl, obviously deformed, lying on a bean bag, making animal sounds toward me as I walked in. I smiled and spoke; later I asked about her. She had been born normal, but had been *beaten* into a vegetable by her *mother!* She was four years old and would never develop; she wasn't even capable of the therapy that most children her age had at a nearby school. And she had been normal.

Another child became so upset when his normal parents visited that it took usually three weeks of love in the Sperling home to sedate him! They had requested that he not leave the home with his parents anymore because he regressed so when with them.

I asked if *any* parents really loved their children. Mrs. Sperling responded that once in a while a child would come from a home full of love, as Justin had, and the parents would visit, love, and care for him. Usually, though, the visits got

49

sparser as time went by. Good intentions have a way of fading.

I soon learned that each of these "unlovable" children was an object of love and a source of pride to their keepers. The entire family joined in with their care, and the neighborhood children visited to help with them.

Children are so beautiful and teach us so many lessons. I had worried about what it would do to Jeff to see these very deformed children making funny sounds as we walked in the room, but the neighbor children, often teenagers, came in just to love them. I told Jeff the children's names and that Jesus loved them individually and that they lived with his brother, Justin. Jeff, too, responded with love! Children accept whatever we allow them to. I also prayed that what Jeff was seeing would serve to make him a better, more compassionate person rather than to have a negative impact on him. I don't know how much of this he will remember later in life, but I do know that he has an insight and compassion for people of all ages that is far beyond his years.

Sometimes I'm overwhelmed at life's inequities! We wanted a normal, healthy child; he would be a vegetable all his life. Other people abuse their normal, healthy children and make vegetables out of them—both physically and emotionally. Surprisingly, though, it wasn't jealousy that overwhelmed me—it was compassion: compassion for the unwanted child who had been so abused; and compassion for the parent with such a warped life that overdosing and child abuse had erupted. This was an ugliness that I had never seen before. I had heard of it but remained untouched. Now, firsthand, I could see how desperately man needs something and Someone he can depend on. How he needs a Savior who can take this warped sense of direction and bring good from it! God had taught me that I was not, out of self-pity, to judge. Now He was replacing that self-pity with compassion. I could actually pray that His love would reach these parents so that they could discover a better way.

The Sperling home that I had earlier launched out against because it "smelled of smoke," on closer inspection actually radiated the love of God! It was Mrs. Sperling's words of faith—"I just *know* he's going to be okay. I work with children like this. Don't you listen to them doctors! God's going to take care of him. I just know it!"—that became my first source of inspiration. I am so embarrassed now to think that I had been so self-righteous and legalistic that I couldn't see God's love at work because of my own prejudice.

9

Justin's Miracle

This plan of mine is not what you would work out, neither are my thoughts the same as yours! For just as the heavens are higher than the earth, so are my ways higher than yours, and my thoughts than yours (Isa. 55:8-9, TLB).

I just couldn't let go! I called or visited daily, feeling all the while that I was imposing on another family to see my child. They were very gracious and very glad I cared, but I couldn't let go *or* feel free. We had so many visitors who wanted to see him. Jeff needed to see his brother and was so proud. Children seem to see through the eyes of love straight to the heart. The deformities that were so ugly to me were accepted, overlooked, and loved by Jeff.

On Friday morning, Mama was to arrive. I called to see how Justin was doing and to make arrangements to have him at home for a few hours for Mama to see him. To my surprise, Mrs. Sperling said, "He's just doing fine! He's sucking now and cries to let us know he's hungry. I just know God's going to heal him! He's going to be okay!"

Do you know the agony of mixed emotions? He was doing better! We had been praying that God would see fit to take him to heaven—and he was improving. God could choose to heal him. We were thrilled! But—he was so healthy that he could live to be a 40-year-old *vegetable!* We couldn't bear the thoughts of that! And he was crying when hungry, but we had elected not to medicate him. If he could feel hunger, he could feel pain, and we couldn't let him suffer. In the hospital, we had to pry his mouth open and pump the nipple to feed him—he couldn't suck; he never cried. Now he was crying *and* sucking. We were trying so hard to let him die, but he was demanding his right to live! I agonized for a while, but finally I whispered a prayer and got on the phone to the doctor.

Dr. Weinberg told me that there was not *one* chance in a *million* that Justin had *any* brain tissue—but there wasn't much more of a chance that he would even be alive today. Of all severe hydrocephalics, 80 percent die within the first week of life (news to us); Justin's chances were even slimmer because his head sores from draining fluid for delivery had been unmedicated. He, medically speaking, should have developed spinal meningitis and died—but his sores had healed themselves and he was improving! Dr. Weinberg said, "Just the fact that he is *alive* a week later means we'd better check. Meet me at Children's Hospital as fast as you can get there."

We picked Justin up, praying that God would work through the doctors and technicians to give us a peace about our decision or to reverse it—and that he would give us a sign of what to do. We didn't ask for a "big" miracle—just a "sign" to direct us. The preliminary X rays showed very little brain tissue; we were asked to call that afternoon for a final report. We were saddened but accepted the diagnosis; we had seen the X rays ourselves. We reminded ourselves that Justin belonged to God and that God was in control of his little life. We remembered our prayer and knew that, *although it was not what we had hoped for, we had to trust God with what we had given Him.* We returned home without hope of a changed decision; Jerry gobbled down a sandwich and left for his afternoon appointments. Then the phone rang.

The hospital asked us to return for more X rays. Somewhat puzzled, we left Mama babysitting the older children; Velda, Laurie, Justin, and I returned. Moments later, we were asked to drop by Dr. Weinberg's office on our way home. We spent an hour and a half in his office, undisturbed. Never, before nor since, have I seen his office without a crowd waiting for him. God took care of *all* the details. Even my active niece, Laurie, took a nap while we talked.

When the technician had enlarged the X rays, he discovered the brain tissue beginning to enlarge toward the top. He called us back for an X ray across the top of Justin's head and discovered 1½ centimeters of brain tissue! To have had such a precise, conscientious technician was, in our eyes, a miracle. Truly God was watching out for us. With less than 1½ centimeters, they could tell us he would be a vegetable; at 1½ centimeters, he might still be—but there is a good chance he can be trainable—and a *minute, small* chance he can be *normal!*

I know I didn't really hear any other word! *Normal!* No one wanted to build up our hopes—but he *could* be *normal!* And he had far more than a minute chance—for he belonged to God, and with God, *all* things are *possible.* And I was very afraid to think of "trainable"—there is a wide range of retardation that is called trainable—and in some ways, to be a vegetable would be better. Society is cruel to a "trainable." I feared deeply that my son would be smart enough to know that he wasn't normal—a pathetic way of life! I vowed that, if God chose to heal him, he would *always* be regarded as normal—or bright—and, whenever possible, treated that way.

What mixed emotions! I had so psyched myself up that Justin was to die; now I wasn't sure how I felt about the X rays. If they had shown normal tissue, we would have immediately praised God for his healing—but we hadn't even

54

asked God for that. We had just asked Him for guidance—for a sign to tell us what direction we should take. To be excited and hope made us vulnerable to more hurt. I was so numb I couldn't think. I probably would still be sitting, stunned, in the doctor's office—but the Lord had sent Velda along to ask questions and think for me. He is so very good—He took care of *all* the details!

Finally, the doctor said: "He's shown us he's going to fight for his life! We owe him *every* chance possible to succeed. I recommend we shunt this baby and give him *every* medical help available. Admit him immediately in Children's Hospital." Could this be the same doctor who, almost to the hour, one week earlier, had considered shunting unethical? Again, he wanted a consultation, but he began immediately treating Justin's jaundice and tapping the fluid on his head.

Needless to say I had a big surprise awaiting Jerry when he arrived home that night! And we both had such mixed emotions! When you've psyched yourself up enough to let go of someone, you are almost speechless and numb when you don't have to. We weren't sure the doctor's news was good, because without the touch of God, we could be prolonging the life of a vegetable. "Trainable" could be pathetic. We had to sit back and remember our prayers—and then, by simple, blind faith, believe that God would surely do His part. We had prayed that He would guide the doctors and X ray technicians to give us a sign. We had to believe that God Almighty had a hand in the discovery of brain tissue. Surely it was the Great Physician reading those X rays. We did not expect an overnight miracle, although God does sometimes work that way. Our vision at this point was of a slow, lifetime healing process—a growth into health.

We knew, too, that God could choose to wait until our son reached heaven for complete healing—that he might, on earth, be "trainable." We had to turn Justin so completely over to God that we could face that possibility. That is not easy! To accept our own shortcomings is one thing—we know we deserve them. But to face handicap in a child that we had created is quite another story. To admit that he would never reach the heights that we had designed for him. That was hard! We realized that we would never really be content with that. We would continue to pray for God's complete touch on his life as long as he lived. We would go on seeking medical and divine guidance for as long as he lived. We would continue to grasp at every hope available for as long as he lived.

We began to realize how God must see us. We fall so short of the plan He has for our lives. We who have been created by a perfect God who has plans and dreams for us are so very less than perfect! He loves us, whether or not we return His love—and we do it by choice. We can elect to serve Him or to mock Him—but He never quits loving us and rooting for us and visualizing us as we can someday become, by His grace and power.

Next came the guilt trip. If our child was to be normal, what had we done to him in the week he had already lived? Even a healthy child will die without stimulation—without colors to look at, things to touch, being touched and loved. Justin had only a slim chance with so many strikes against him. Now he was under the belly lights to treat his jaundice, and we couldn't hold him for very long. He heard few sounds for stimulation. He saw only white, white, white. And we could spend so little time with him—we had Jeff, baby-sitters, jobs! Guilt set in when I left Justin to be with Jeff; guilt set in when I left Jeff to be with Justin; guilt set in when I thought of having already given him a week out of our home—even though I knew that I could not have cared for him as the Sperlings had—either physically or emotionally.

I cried to God again: "God, I need to be helping him and I can't. He'll never make it! He doesn't have me there beside him. He needs to be held and loved and cuddled—and we can't! He needs to see colors, and everything is white. He needs to hear sounds, and the hospital is so quiet. He'll never make it!"

Then that sweet peace and power that I learned to depend on literally filled my frightened body—and God replied, through His "still small voice," "Can you trust Me for the 'little things'? If I can create a brain, I can repair it! If I would elect to repair his brain, give him life and health, don't you think I would also take care of the details?"

God didn't scold me for doubting. He just gave me peace. Then He showed me that He had already taken care of the things I'd just begun to worry about. I asked His forgiveness for my lack of faith—and I asked Him for more faith—and I told Him I would trust Justin's development into his care. We walked into the hospital just hours later where we found a nurse rocking Justin. It wasn't feeding time or changing time—she was just loving him! When she saw us, she reluctantly gave him to us, telling us how she loved him. Then she told us that he was already a favorite, because they sensed he was, indeed, a miracle child. A group of Christian nurses gathered around him to pray for him at the end of each shift.

Isn't that just like God? He had taken care of the details before I even thought to pray about them! He let the nurses have a special quality of love to give when his mother, afraid of giving herself completely for fear of hurting more, was also very obligated to another child who desperately needed an overdose of love and security right now. I had heard "Jesus doeth *all* things well" all my life—I had just learned that it was true! He is at work in our lives whenever we call on Him, even when we cannot see or feel it! In His goodness, He let me see His hand at work through Justin's life. Surely He is just as at work in my life today. Surely He is answering our prayers because He loves us, even before we know to call on Him.

Need I say that Justin's jaundice healed *very* quickly? Dr. Bonner, the neurosurgeon, read the X rays, reversed his earlier decision, and prepared to operate. He talked at length with us about his prospects; I am still thankful that he was so willing to care for our entire family! His schedule was so busy that he would often call us between 11 p.m. and 1 a.m. In spite of the hour, he always had time to explain things. We could freely say, "I don't know what that means. Explain it in nonmedical terms"; and he would kindly do it, always saying before he hung up, "Are you sure you have no more questions?"

Dr. Bonner was highly recommended; we prayed for God's guidance and felt completely confident that we were in the right hands. God so often reassured us during our tough times. Shortly after Justin's first surgery, we learned that Dr. Bonner had trained the Southern California surgeon who had been recommended to us as "one of the best." We were confident that God had selected our physicians.

Dr. Bonner stated some frightening facts before the surgery. We had no guarantees of the outcome. Justin's potential ranged, still, from a vegetable to a normal child—with both extremes being very slim. Where there was hope, we must take it. Both doctors agreed that we did not have a choice—we had to try. We had to give our "little fighter" every chance possible to succeed. He also stated, though, that Justin's chances of pulling through major surgery were not good; he was not a strong child, and putting any child under anesthesia was risky. We could be ending his life through surgery; we could be prolonging the life of a vegetable if he survived but didn't have any brain capacity. With this word, we faced at least a two-hour major surgery somewhat numb!

Operation day came. I believe that divine healing takes

place in an operating room *every* time a patient survives and recovers. I was not at all in question about whether to operate or whether to pray for the touch of God. If Justin survived, God indeed would have touched. God uses surgeons and doctors to do His healing—and without the healing touch of God, a doctor is powerless. The doctors told us many times during Justin's lifetime how unpredictable human life is. A patient with all vital signs looking good will die; a patient will be given up for dead, medically speaking, and will survive with a great potential. A trained physician does all that he can do; the rest is up to a greater power. That Power is no respecter of persons—He causes the sun to shine on the just and the unjust. If He caused it to shine only on the just, there would be few of us with health today!

As we faced the surgery, we realized that God could elect to take Justin to heaven through the surgery and that, if He did, Justin would indeed be healed. We faced operation day knowing that God was in control—knowing that His will had been prayed for and that Justin belonged to Him, and that, whatever the outcome, it would "work together for good."

We walked down the hallway with Justin as far as they would let us go. We asked our pastor, Orville, to pray with us and he prayed a beautiful dedication prayer before they wheeled Justin into surgery; I prayed that prayer with him in my heart. He prayed that Jesus would go where we couldn't; that the hands of the Great Physician would guide the hands of the surgeon; that God would be glorified through the surgery, no matter what the outcome; that we would have a deep sense of peace knowing that Jesus, who loved Justin far more than we did, was there caring for him; and that, whatever the outcome, we would accept it as the will of God.

Oh, how it hurt to walk away! But our confidence in God surged deeper than the hurt! God himself was in that surgery room; He was also there with me, giving comfort and peace during the long two hours plus that were to follow.

At last, Dr. Bonner walked into the waiting room. We hardly recognized him in his "operation garb." He told us that Justin had survived the surgery miraculously! His body was accepting the shunt now—often a body will reject any foreign object, making such a surgery unsuccessful. The shunt was working well; he was recovering rapidly. The fluid was high in protein which made it sticky. There was a chance that the shunt would clog somewhere down the line, but at the moment all was well. He would be in recovery for an hour; then we could see him.

Can you imagine the faces on a group of people who really expected, fearfully, to hear that their baby was in heaven? The waiting room was full—in addition to Jerry and me, Orville had remained with us; Bill and Velda were there; Alton and Margie, my adopted parents, were there. We all rushed up to the surgeon, preparing ourselves for bad news. We burst into tears of joy! God, indeed, had touched both Dr. Bonner's hands and our baby! Margie stated it best: "We should have known! After all, he was in the hands of the Great Physician! How could we have expected anything other than a miracle!" And again, we were reminded, "Jesus doeth *all* things well."

An hour later, we were startled again. We walked in to see a baby that had just had a two-hour major surgery on his brain. He had been weak before surgery started; recovery in a healthy child takes 6 to 10 days; it might take weeks for him because he was so tiny and weak. After surgery, a healthy person is groggy. We walked in, bracing ourselves to see suffering. We looked into the bright, big, healthy eyes of a baby, still in some pain, eyeing his surroundings and responding to our touch of love! This wasn't even the same child that had gone into surgery. The eyes that had never before appeared to see were looking around. The God of the universe had touched him! Without doubt, we knew that God had His hand on our child, and we realized how deeply unworthy we were of His goodness.

We had received as a gift shortly after Justin's birth a book, *Psalms of My Life*, by Joseph Bayly. We returned home from the hospital to read the one that became so dear to us during Justin's lifetime. His words express so beautifully our feelings:

A Psalm at Children's Hospital

I find it hard Lord
agonizing hard
to stand here
looking through the glass
at this my infant son.
What suffering
is in this world
to go through pain of birth
and then through
pain of knife
within the day.
What suffering
is in the world
this never ending
pain parade
to death.
He moves
a bit
not much
how could an infant
stuffed with tubes
cut sewed and bandaged
move more than that?

Some day he'll shout
and run a race
roll down a grassy hill
ice skate
on frosty night like this.
He'll sing
and laugh
I know he will Lord.
But if not
if You should take him home
to Your home
help me then remember
how Your Son suffered
and You stood by
watching
agonizing watching
waiting
to bring all suffering to an end
forever
on a day
yet to be.
Look Lord
he sleeps.
I must go now.
Thank You for staying
Nearer than oxygen
than dripping plasma
to my son.
Please be that near
to mother
sister brothers
and to me.*

*From *Psalms of My Life,* by Joseph Bayly (Wheaton, Ill.: Tyndale House Publishers, Inc., © 1969). Used by permission.

And He was that near to each of us! Somehow we had a deep confidence that we were being touched by God and that *whatever* happened would be okay. We also knew that God's plans and ways were much higher than ours and that we could not understand what was happening. Our perspectives are so earthy. We realized that there were depths we could not see as we watched God's touch on the life of our son.

10

We Couldn't Ask More

*If you want to know what God wants you to do, ask
him, and he will gladly tell you, for he is always ready
to give a bountiful supply of wisdom to all who ask
him; he will not resent it* (Jas. 1:5, TLB).

A new decision faced us; the new circumstances had
changed the earlier facts with which we had decided to place
Justin in the Sperling home. Inconceivable as it may be, we
had to labor over the decision again. Perhaps it seems natural
that we would just take Justin home and praise God for his
healing. But . . .

Days earlier we had chosen to allow someone else to
care for our child who would be mentally and physically
incapable all his life—without human hope. We made that
decision knowing that "With God *all* things are possible." We
made it knowing that we could reverse it at any time. We
made it, too, on the practical advice of Christian friends who
had seen the emotional, physical, and financial drain that a
handicapped child had made on the lives of other very dedicated Christian people who also knew that God was in the
healing business and who prayed daily and praised daily for
the physical healing of their child. We could not really let go
of our child in that situation—but we made the decision that
we felt was best under the circumstances. This decision was
affirmed by our ministers and Christian friends who worked
with handicapped people; their support helped.

I don't understand the healing of God. Sometimes He touches a hopeless life and gives it health. I know, too, that there are many hopelessly handicapped who, for some reason, God has chosen not to heal on earth, and they have friends and loved ones who continue to trust God and to pray daily for their healing. When we look for God's touch, we must be willing to leave the decision completely in His hands; then pray for His guidance in what we are to do.

Now we were haunted again! The facts had all changed! Things were even more uncertain now than they had been before, for there is a *huge* gap between vegetable and normal. The more we talked with people who work with handicapped or retarded children, the more we were excited at Justin's possibilities. But the more we learned, the more we realized our inadequacies. I didn't have the confidence in training a normal child to utilize his capabilities to the best of his potential; so I was at a total loss at the thought of stimulating a child that needed special attention. I could work with a drug addict or an emotional problem and feel at least like I knew what direction to head; but I didn't really even know what it meant to "stimulate" a baby, and I would become so discouraged if I didn't see progress.

What was best for Justin? We had to do what was best for him. God had indeed touched him; we had to do our part. But how does one know what that "part" is? Would he, in the long run, develop to a greater capacity in a home equipped to stimulate him, with people who had a special knowledge and gift that I didn't have? Or would he, in the long run, develop to a greater capacity just because he knew he had the love of mother, father, brother, friends? Would love outweigh the advantages that a full-time therapist could give?

These thoughts may sound minor now, but they were torture then. To reverse our decision was to take on a frightening responsibility. I needed time alone while raising my normal child. The thoughts of constant pressure that a handicapped child, even with the touch of God, would bring into our home, were staggering. We prayed for divine guidance, and the confusion grew.

We spent the week of Justin's recovery counseling with doctors, ministers, and friends who worked with handicapped people. We read books and articles from parents who had had similar experiences; some elected to place or institutionalize their children; some elected to keep them at home for care. They told their experiences and emotional adjustments to their situation. There were definite advantages to each decision, which left us, again, in a dilemma.

Our friends spent countless hours listening to our cries. When they were professionally knowledgeable, they shared their insight, but they refused to make our decision for us. They listened without criticism and with compassion; they assured us that they would back whatever decision we chose to make, without condemnation. They assured us that they didn't know what decision they would make in a similar circumstance, and they let us know that they loved us! Could we have asked for more? We felt a deep security that friends cared and that they would not condemn us, whatever we decided. Christian fellowship is a gift of God!

Justin recovered rapidly! Normal shunt surgery takes from 6 to 10 days; the doctors had expected Justin to take longer for recovery. The fifth day after surgery they told us he would be released the following day! That was the same day we had an appointment with the doctor from the Central Valley Regional Center to discuss Justin and to try to make our decision on what to do. Somehow, in the midst of our confusion on what to do, we had been praying that this doctor would have our answer, that he would say something that would lead us in the right direction. When we learned that Justin was to be released the morning *before* our appointment that afternoon, we felt a sense of panic. Then a deep confidence and peace set in. God had never sent us an answer too late before; He could be trusted now to clear our minds and remove the confusion when the time came for our decision. Almost immediately following releasing this problem to God's timing, we learned that Justin would have to return to the Sperling home at least for one day following his release in order to have the medical expenses underwritten without question and without having to redo all the paper work to change budget classification. You see, God's answers are never too late!

We prayed before arriving at the regional center that God would remove our confusion and give us a definite answer. We sensed that we would have to do what was best for Justin, so we also prayed that God would take care of the rest of us once the decision was made. The doctor there began to relate the facts about Justin to us—identically as the facts had been related by every other doctor. I whispered, "Lord, I need answers! Clear our minds!" Then we asked the direct question: "Where will Justin be better off? In a home without knowledge, but where he is loved and valued—or in a home where he can receive the extra stimulation and training he needs?"

Without question and without hesitation the doctor replied: "In a home where he is loved! There is no question about it. The other is an alternative—and a good one—and should be used if there is friction in the home or if he creates stress that is damaging to the family members; but *any* child is better off where he is loved!"

His answer sent us the peace that we needed; we would—*gladly, thankfully*—take our son home! But that wasn't all God had to say to us through him; the decision was made, then he told us more . . .

The regional center would send a therapist into our

home as often as once a week, if needed, to work with Justin and to train me.

The regional center would provide a baby-sitter trained to work with handicapped children, to come into our home to care for Justin from one hour up to one day when I (or we) reached the point where pressures had built up and I needed to get away for a while. There's more!

The regional center would help us with placement for up to one month if we wanted a vacation and felt he couldn't benefit from the trip or travel. There's more!

The regional center would put us in contact with people who worked with handicapped children so we could visit and learn from them and share our frustrations with someone who could provide practical advice. There's more!

With our current income level, there would be *no charge to us* for any of these services!

We had never even considered the fact that we could have it all—love, stimulation, *and* professional advice. Our finances wouldn't allow a teen baby-sitter more often than twice a month. Our deepest prayers were answered, even though we didn't know enough to pray them.

Just in case you've been wondering—*Jesus doeth all things well!*

11

Justin Comes Home!

For the Lord is always good. He is always loving and kind, and his faithfulness goes on and on to each succeeding generation (Ps. 100:5, TLB).

Our baby came home! There is no joy that compares to bringing home your newborn! There is no hurt quite like having to leave your child in the hospital, for whatever reason. There is no agony quite like that of leaving a child you have loved and planned for, never to bring him home.

Contrast that, then, with the jubilant, happy, joyful, grateful people who, just two weeks after their child had been condemned to die, got to bring him home! Unpacking the clothes we had packed in sorrow just days earlier was cause for celebration. I don't know who was the most excited. Jeff ran in, just minutes after we got home, saying, "Mom, could Justin come outside and play ball?" Then he grabbed his hand and said, "Come on, Justin! Let's play football!" holding up his little football for Justin to see. We became a family of four for just a few short weeks; when I look back on the love we shared, I am deeply grateful God sent him home.

Justin developed remarkably. When we brought him home, he couldn't move his head when lying on his back. Days later, with effort, he could move his head from side to side when on his stomach. He lay perfectly still at first. We all took part in exercising his arms and legs. Jeff learned how to "stimulate" his baby brother and beamed with pride at being a good helper. Then we watched Justin as he, so slowly and precisely, began to move—first arms, then legs. Those were exciting days! His accomplishments were so major. Things that I had taken for granted in Jeff's development were a whole day's work for Justin. We applauded him as he struggled.

One day, I looked for an odor (I have one of those noses!). Finally I found it! Dead skin in Justin's clenched fist. I found the same thing in his toes that were tense. As I massaged and cleaned his hands and feet, he gradually began to open them—starting with his little finger and, finger by finger, working his way to his thumb. When the therapist visited the first week, she explained that this was one sign of a sick, tense child. They must first learn to relax and open their hands (a direct response to love and stimulation). Then, in the opposite sequence (thumb first), they learn to grasp. I think Jeff was born grasping! Development is such a miracle and we take it so for granted.

Justin liked the orange and white polka-dot giraffes on his wallpaper. He watched his mobile. This was so exciting! The doctors and therapists had feared for his eyesight. He could see! Shortly after that he looked into my eyes as I talked to him, indicating he could really see. Jeff gave me a good "looking over" with his big, beautiful, expressive eyes the first time I ever held him, but Justin had to learn to focus his eyes before he could look into mine. The therapist explained, again, that there is a sequential visual pattern of development. First a baby sees a repeated design; that he had recognized and responded to the polka dots was good news. Then he responds to a face; the progression was good news. Next, his eyes would learn to follow movement. And they did! Within weeks, he definitely turned his head to follow me around the room when someone else was holding him. In our normal children, we take their development for granted and don't even realize it's happening. Life is really a miracle. That most children are born normal and without handicap is the greatest miracle of all.

During this time, God gave me a vision to be thankful for my many blessings rather than to cry over my hardships. This is not normal for me—it was a direct gift from God to help me through. While I was watching Justin develop, I was praising God for his development *and* for the fact God had created such a fascinating system of life. I was praising God that Jeff had been healthy and that most children are healthy. I realized that life and health are God's gifts.

God responds to our needs—and when things come our way that humanly we can't bear, He fills us with a special capacity to make it through. I think of this as the "calm in the midst of the storm," or the "peace that passes understanding." Humanly speaking, we should have complained about our child's prospects, but God opened our eyes to see His hand-iwork in Justin's life. In spite of handicap, when God touches, there is beauty and goodness.

The Bible says that all goodness comes from God. I do not believe that God sent a handicapped baby into our world to test us! If God is good, He is not the creator of the bad! He can test us and build our faith without having to use our petty ways. I believe that *all* sickness and *all* handicap and *all* things less than perfect are in our world because of the influence of Satan. The only things that God sends are the good things! *All* healing and *all* health and *all* beauty come from God, our Creator. God allows sickness and handicap and evil because He has given us a free will and because sin rules our world. Christians are subject to all the forces of evil while they live in this world. God rarely steps in to change that fact, but He always goes through our tough places with us, giving us strength and support. And once in a while, in His goodness, He lifts us out of the sinful world and lets us really get a glimpse of Him!

This happened to me during Justin's lifetime. He did not change my circumstances and give complete healing, but He did touch my life and my heart. He gave me peace and joy in the midst of my situation, and many times during these months, He allowed me to see my situation from His eyes. My perspectives are so different than His! I couldn't imagine God being glorified through a handicapped life unless He chose to touch in total healing. But God let me see that *He doesn't need health to have glory.* And *always,* if we will give the things we have tainted by sin or the things life has handed to us deformed and warped to the One who created life in the first place, He will *work it together for good!* He had promised us that—and if He is God, He can't break His promise. He has told us that He is good—and we must believe in His integrity and know that only goodness can come to us from His hand.

Usually God gives us sight of His work as we look back. Usually we can't see His "working together" as we face a storm or before it comes—but *always* He will work things out if we allow Him freedom to work, because He loves us.

12

God's Healing Touch

The joy of the Lord is your strength (Neh. 8:10).

Wherever you go with a baby, people stop and look! I realized that Justin would respond to the way other people saw him. I wanted him to grow up proud, self-confident, loved. I did not want him to grow up thinking of himself as "less than perfect" and, most of all, I did not want him to grow up wallowing in self-pity. When we went out, people saw the scar on his head and the lump where his shunt was placed and his shaved head. The normal human reaction to a handicapped child is either to look and then quickly turn away, avoiding the handicap; or to pity, usually saying something like, "Poor thing. What's wrong?"

With my very friendly Jeff, people everywhere were drawn to him. In fact, shopping with a baby was a real education to me. I was used to running in and out of a store quickly; when I shopped with Jeff, every time I turned a corner, someone else was looking at and talking to the baby. I think Jeff is such an outgoing child because people everywhere, whether they knew him or not, were drawn to him, talked to him, played with him, and loved him. Like most babies, he became so accustomed to being noticed that he would pick out total strangers and begin smiling at them and reaching for them to take him. People, by their actions, say to a normal child, "You're cute. You're fun to be with. You're worthwhile. I love you." By their actions they say to a handicapped child, "It's a shame you have to be that way! I feel sorry for you. You'll have a sad life." While we wouldn't say these things, we speak so loudly by the way we act.

Pity is an insult! Most of us feel uncomfortable around "different" people. We avoid them because we don't know what to say. Because of Justin, I am learning. Now I admire people who bravely face a life of hardship, and I am ashamed of my past feelings.

However, we must all accept life as it is. The reality was that people responded to Justin out of fear and pity because they didn't know any better. We decided to take preventive action. Justin was a beautiful child. People were drawn to him—rushed to look closer—and seeing the shunt and scar, were overwhelmed by pity—and retreated. So I covered the scar! Everywhere we went, my Bicentennial baby wore a cute little red, white, and blue cap. People who rushed to see him responded with love to his beauty. When they learned of his handicap, they said by their reactions, "This child is a miracle! God has touched him! He is worthwhile!" And they verbally responded either, "I'll be praying for your boy! God will continue to touch him"; or, "I've been so unfaithful to God! I'm going to make some changes in my own life as a result of hearing this."

Oh, that we might respond to *every* child, normal and handicapped, with this beautiful attitude. Justin could not possibly grow up pitying himself when everyone he met radiated with love and spoke of the goodness of God!

I think it's important to mention that Justin's "cap" did not make us pretend that his handicap was nonexistent. For some reason, God demands that we face our situations in total honesty; He would not have blessed if we had refused to believe the doctors. We had to accept Justin's condition and love him *as he was*. And God asks us to do that to everyone

74

we meet. The cap served as a shield from a cruel world and as an open door to praise God.

It was very hard to compare Justin's progress only to Justin—to measure his progress by yesterday rather than by charts and friends. Discouragement and discontent came only when we failed to look at him as an individual and began comparing him to other children.

We took Justin everywhere with us, treating him as one of the family, which he definitely was. In Jeff's eyes and attitude were pride, acceptance, and love. Justin went shopping, out to eat, to the zoo, to church. We allowed people to love him—and we *finally* allowed ourselves to love him, unconditionally. It's hard to confess that you can love your children by choosing to do so—but as I've stated earlier, we realized that if we loved, we would hurt. We had to come to the place where we would take that chance. From the moment we made our decision to bring him home and "try," we chose to love him unconditionally—and we did. We chose to pray daily that God would completely touch his body in human healing—but we chose to love him deeply, as every parent should love his child, regardless of his human potential. That love was very small compared to the joy his little life gave us in return! We continued to pray that God would love through Justin's life and would bring good, and God gave us a spirit of joy as we faced each day.

I don't think I realized that a parent could choose whether to invest himself in his child or not. It really frightens me when I think that I almost cheated myself out of loving my baby! We get so busy "living" our lives that we sometimes just forget what life is all about.

People everywhere were attracted to Justin. I was aware that God touched people often through him. They would look at the baby, ask questions, and immediately praise God. In a doctor's office one day, a lady slipped me a piece of paper as she left. On it was written, "Repeat this every day: I see Justin as God sees Justin—perfect in mind and body. It works!" She had shared with me her own son's battle to overcome brain damage—he is now a CPA—and had promised to pray for us. A friend in Bible Study Fellowship shared with me that she had accepted Christ as her Savior because of the way she had seen God care for us during Justin's life. She had been watching people and contemplating her decision throughout the Bible study. Then she saw a life shielded by God—and because of Justin made her choice for heaven. God began to show me how wrong my perspectives had been, how limited my vision! It doesn't matter what our intellectual or physical capacities are—if we are responsible for leading one person to Christ, our lives are worthwhile. Justin had already had a more worthwhile life than many people because he had been used of God!

It is not normal for me to meet strangers on the street and begin talking about God, but when people would look at Justin and be strangely drawn to him, no matter how hard I tried to keep quiet, the joy of what God was doing in my life just bubbled out. Even "hard"-appearing people would say, "I've got so much to be thankful for! My children are normal. God has been so good to me, and I didn't even realize it!" One person used almost those very words as he buried the *Playboy* magazine he was reading and remembered how he loved his wife.

We can use life's problems to present a positive attitude and to praise God that He'll take us through. Sometimes people with handicapped children shield them and hide them, embarrassed and ashamed. They apologize for them, feeling they must explain their child's condition to everyone they meet. I understand this—I've been there—but it's so wrong!

We became more outgoing and more willing to praise God as we walked through our days. We didn't have to praise God for His healing touch. We praised Him because He was good and was giving us joy and was caring for us and was helping us. Nothing about our praise was fake, and nothing about our praise served to manipulate God into completely touching our child. Our hearts were filled with joy regardless of Justin's potential. I believe that attitude was a gift to us from God.

I was visiting with a friend one day, sharing with her Justin's development. While I could easily praise God for what He had done and for who He is, I could never assume He had chosen to heal Justin completely and could never believe that Justin was normal. I could believe that God had the power to heal, but could not testify that the work was done without visual evidence. I would always pray that God would touch completely and help Justin develop into normality. My friend said, "You have to praise God that the healing has been done. Not to praise God keeps Him from actually doing the work. Of course, He's going to heal. Praise Him for it!"

This statement sent me to my knees in guilt. Was my lack of faith keeping God from healing my son? When I have seen a physical healing, I have known without doubt that God has acted. God has given me the faith that my prayers were answered. I didn't have this assurance that God had totally healed Justin. Was I to fake what I didn't have? Was God's power, indeed, dependent upon my praise for release? How I labored over this! As I cried, God spoke to me, as He did so tenderly throughout Justin's lifetime: "Faith is a gift of God." I couldn't fake what I didn't have.

Then God softly whispered to me, "Justin's life belongs in *My* hands, not yours." Nothing that I could do would heal him—including praise. My son belonged to Jesus! I would love him as long as Jesus gave me life; I would pray for God's healing touch on his mind and body as long as God gave him life—but *I would not attempt to manipulate God*, and I would not attempt to play God. Justin's healing was in the hands of God, to be done in God's timing, and to be done in God's way. If I was to claim healing in praise to God, God would give me the faith to do so.

I don't understand healing. As I read the Bible, I see that Jesus healed *all* who came to Him. We have healing available to us today—and God does heal many times when we don't recognize it and don't give Him credit. *Every* time healing occurs, it is because God has touched. God created the normal body process that repairs a skinned knee; God touches through the hands of a successful surgery; God gives a new body and new life when a soul goes to heaven. Wherever there is life and health, God has touched.

One way that God heals is to give us joy in the midst of our struggles. God healed me as well as Justin.

13

Troubles Come in Bundles

*Come unto me, all ye that labour and are heavy laden,
and I will give you rest* (Matt. 11:28).

We were rapidly reaching the place of physical and emotional exhaustion and planned a vacation for the upcoming holiday weekend. A week before we were to leave, we received word that Daboy, my grandfather, was dying. Panic always sets in when death threatens one you love. I was glad I didn't have any apologies left unsaid, but Daboy had raised me, and I needed to tell him again how I loved him.

I'm not afraid to die, but I don't want to. God created us with an uncanny will to live, and He is pleased when we enjoy the life He has given us. But we tend to argue with Him when death threatens us or one we love. Telling God He was surely doing things wrong and we didn't need this now, we changed our much-needed vacation into a trip home. I flew, and Jerry joined me a week later. We prayed that Daboy would live until we got there and asked God to give us, in the midst of the confusion that always sets in when a loved one is suffering, the retreat we so desperately needed.

The day before I was to leave, I took Justin in for his regular pediatric checkup. That was followed by an emergency trip to the surgeon's office, because of the frantic news that Justin's head had enlarged. We knew that if his shunt had clogged, we would cancel our trip—but we prayed again that God would care for him *and* allow us to be with Daboy. And God answered our prayer. The surgeon showed me how to pump Justin's shunt to keep it flushed out. It was sluggish from the high protein, but it wasn't clogged. He told me what to watch for in case the shunt should clog. Then he told me to catch my plane and enjoy my trip.

Daboy was alive when we got there, but he was in intensive care and could only be seen for minutes at a time. He was semiconscious only once when I visited; other times, he didn't appear to know I was there. His precious words when Justin was born came back to me. I wanted so badly to tell him Justin was doing great. We don't know what to say when people are dying. I wanted to say, "Daboy, when you get to heaven . . ." and I wanted to say, "I'll see you again someday." But I couldn't say that. I told him how much we loved him and needed him and wanted him to fight for his life. I knew he was dying, but I didn't want him to.

Suddenly, Jeff's eyes crossed! Another emergency room, panic-stricken! We spent hours in hospital waiting rooms. But as the pressures mounted from the outside: Daboy's illness, Justin's setback, Jeff's eye problem—strength mounted up from within. God blessed and rested us, just as we had asked Him to. In addition to that, Jerry and I finally were able to leave our boys with his family and get away for two days. We needed time alone, away from our pressures, even more than we needed the "family vacation" that we had planned.

About a week later, the boys and I returned for Daboy's funeral. Our extended families got a chance to see and love our "miracle baby," and none of us realized it would be the only time they would see him alive. Was I ashamed of his handicap? Not one whit. God had, indeed, touched *my* life with pride.

As to rest, I got what I needed and more. God gave me the assurance of the multitude of prayers, love, and support emerging from the hearts of relatives and friends who lived many miles from my home.

14

Justin's Dedication

I want you to trust me in your times of trouble, so I can rescue you, and you can give me glory (Ps. 50:15, TLB).

We grew to love our little boy more every day. We prayed more fervently every day that God would see fit to totally heal him. We learned so much about handicapped children. I was constantly amazed at what a brain-damaged child could achieve and what medicine could do. I was equally amazed at what medicine still could not do. Medicine could correct a problem such as hydrocephalus, but medicine could not detect it early in a pregnancy, could not repair the damaged tissue left by it, could not estimate the extent of the damage accurately, and did not know what caused it. God remained close to us, and we felt the time had come to reach out in faith and trust Him for Justin's total healing. I had visions of a struggle—but I had visions of success, for God had obviously touched our baby.

We made arrangements to have Justin dedicated shortly after things had settled down from Daboy's funeral. Alton and Margie were on the road to his dedication when problems set in. Justin began having seizures. The doctor prescribed medicine, but the seizures worsened. Within hours, he had regressed. He moved only in pain, and a visit to the doctor confirmed the worst. His shunt had clogged; he would have to have emergency surgery immediately.

Again, we saw Dr. Weinberg in action! Dr. Bonner was

on vacation, and the surgeon taking his calls was unaware of Justin's condition. He planned to hospitalize Justin and wait until the next morning before treating him. Dr. Weinberg was at the hospital when we arrived with Justin. He made a quick phone call, obviously irate over the postponed treatment, and announced that the surgeon would be in immediately, dropping all his other patients until he had cared for Justin. The surgeon did arrive soon; he tapped the fluid and scheduled surgery for early the next morning—almost the very hour of Justin's planned dedication.

It was months later before I realized the cause of Dr. Weinberg's action and the reason for his insistence that the surgeon drop his other patients to care for Justin. If left untreated, a hydrocephalic child dies within 24 to 48 hours after his shunt has clogged. Justin had already gone 24 hours because of my ignorance. The surgeon was not planning to treat at all for another 24! I could see that he was already a "vegetable" again, but had no idea how close we came to losing him. God cared for us through our pediatrician! Had it not been for his care, our baby would have died in the hospital that night awaiting his visit from the surgeon.

Alton and Margie arrived at Velda's late Saturday night. There they heard the shocking news of a surgery to replace the dedication. Early the next morning, they arrived at the hospital with Bill, Velda, and family, to keep the long vigil with us.

We followed our baby down that long hallway again! When we reached the end, we prayed that Jesus would go where we couldn't. This time it hurt so much more. This was our son! We had invested ourselves in his life! We still knew he belonged in the hands of God, but this time our prayers were not, "Lord, have Thy will done"; they were, "Lord, please touch him! Please, make it Your will to touch him!" And the hours of surgery were long and painful. I should be able to say here that I trusted God so much that it didn't matter what the outcome; but when I had risked loving, I had chosen to care. And it *did* matter! Even though I knew God was in control, there was no hesitancy to pray for His healing touch now!The doctors assured us that Justin's chances were much better than they had been two months earlier; he was healthier. But there was still that painful anticipation.

I really think that God wants us to love others this deeply. To love anyone is to risk losing and hurting, but to fail to love is to withdraw and die. Our love is within God's will as long as it does not possess the object of our love or make it into our god. And I learned that God truly understands our hurts as we watch our loved ones suffering.

Justin did pull through that surgery. I was surprised that he did so well—my faith apparently was still on vacation! Usually, death is not anywhere in my thoughts, but I feared his death deeply. I was almost afraid to rejoice when he recovered so rapidly. God did touch him again. God did work through the surgeon. My fear, then, did not come from God—even death is not faced with fear when God is in control.

Our pastors cared for us so beautifully. While we were undergoing emergency surgery, Orville took time in the regular church service to pray for us and to pray for Justin. Our friends told us that we need never doubt that we had, indeed, dedicated Justin. Orville tenderly presented our needs in Christian love to the congregation and prayed a dedication prayer, and everyone there knew that our son was in the hands of the God of the universe before that prayer was over. I wasn't there, but I know that God touched our lives; and I know that our son was, indeed, brought to God in Christian dedication.

As I visited Justin during his days of recovery, I had a terrible feeling that we were losing him. Medically speaking, he was doing fine, but he had regressed so rapidly. I continued to pray for God's touch on his life and began to regret things I had neglected. I had planned to have his picture made, both alone and with Jeff, and had not gotten around to it. We had snapshots, but I wanted a good picture. I was sure now that I would never have it. I didn't even bring my request to God in prayer—I just felt bad because I didn't have that picture.

But Justin *was* released! He recovered again in record time. Needless to say, I hardly allowed him the luxury of home before I rushed him in to have his picture made. However, he had become a "vegetable" again. The photographer worked overtime, because Justin didn't respond to the stimulation and simply tried to sleep. I told her that it was fine if he was sleeping. I would settle for whatever we got and be thankful to have it. The pictures are priceless to me.

As we were leaving the photographer's office, Justin had another seizure. The doctor had assured us that this was normal with any brain-damaged child and that it could be controlled with medication; but oh, it's such agony to watch your child suffer and be so helpless! I have heard that a child does not really suffer during a seizure, but Justin appeared to be suffering, and nothing I could do helped!

The next day I took him to the doctor again because he just didn't seem well. I was frustrated; nothing was apparently wrong, but he just wasn't right. And, as I had feared, we traveled from the doctor's office back to the hospital; Justin had spinal meningitis. He had been home less than 48 hours—and, looking back, I believe he was home just so God could answer that deep prayer of my heart that I hadn't even had the faith to pray—I wanted a good picture of him.

You know, God cares about the "little things." I have heard people say that we shouldn't "bother God" with little things—He's too big and important to waste His time. Nothing could be farther from the truth! The God of the Universe loves me so much that He knows how many hairs I have on my head! He really cares about the "little" things that are important to me. It was important that I have a picture of my son, so He made arrangements for Justin to have two days "away" from his illness so I could have my picture. He cares.

I think that as Christians, we must believe this truth and live by this principle whether or not we can see what God is doing about the details. I know there are many people far more worthy than I who do not have a picture of a child they lost. I know there are many people far more worthy than I who have loved ones living in pathetic conditions. God seems far away and removed from where they are living now—it appears as though He doesn't care. I really *do* know that feeling! I have lived there myself at times. But I *still* believe that God cares about the little things that touch my life—and I *still* believe that all things will work together for good—and I *still* believe that God is working even when I can't see it.

God's promises are true, and we must believe in the love and integrity of God regardless of where we find ourselves. A time will come when again, from my heart, I can say, "Truly, God has been good. He has been here all the time!" I hope that time comes before I get to heaven—but if it doesn't, it will be no less true. We must never forget and never fail to stand in awe at the truth that God loves us and that God loves those we love far more than we do, *whether or not we or they are walking in God's light.* You see, God's love is so much more beautiful than ours could ever be!

I used to say, "When I get to heaven, I'm going to ask God why . . ." And the list was endless. I really think now, though, that when I get to heaven, I won't have to ask God about anything. I think I will just stand in awe, my mind filled with God's wisdom, and wonder how He could love me in spite of my belligerence and lack of faith. I used to read Exodus and wonder why God didn't just zap those ungrateful Israelites off the face of the earth. They had seen His tender, loving care and dynamic protection. He had parted the Red Sea; He had sent them food daily. Then they complained and turned from Him when Moses spent just 40 days away. I no longer wonder—I just stand in awe and thanksgiving that He loves me that much, too.

We did believe, after seeing God's touch on Justin's life, that God would heal him. Through the days, we had written a letter announcing his birth. It was ready to go about the time that Justin was readmitted to the hospital with spinal meningitis. The letter was long, giving all the details; a portion of it follows:

Dear Friends,

Your prayers in our behalf have brought about a miracle! We want to take a moment to say, "Thank you," and to catch you up on all the details.

On April 1, our son, Justin David, was born. He was hydrocephalic. . . . As I type this letter, Justin is in the hospital recovering from emergency shunt revision surgery—but the surgical x rays showed 2½ centimeters of brain tissue! At two weeks of age, he had barely 1½ centimeters, so this news tells us there is growth going on, and he will be *at least* trainable. Praise God!

The letter was never mailed. Justin didn't get better. We spent long days, then long weeks, then long months in the hospital. Did we lose faith in God because He didn't heal as we thought He would? No! Human healing couldn't have done what God did through the sick little body of a baby getting ready to live with Jesus.

15

Thank God Anyway

In every thing give thanks: for this is the will of God in Christ Jesus concerning you (1 Thess. 5:18).

Justin lay in the hospital, getting progressively worse. The days were long and hard. We lived one hour at a time. The doctors tried first one medication, then another. The meningitis continued to flare. Finally, they decided that another surgery was necessary. Justin's infection could not heal with a "foreign object" in his body. The third surgery removed the drain in his shunt so that it drained outside rather than inside his body.

Still, the infection gained ground. His fourth surgery was to remove the remains of both shunts, completely ridding his body of the "foreign object." This meant, however, that his head had to be "tapped" daily to remove the excess fluid. In the process, a needle was inserted into the soft spot on top of his head to withdraw the fluid that had built up pressure. Following this procedure, he could not be held for several hours, or he would go into a state of shock. Much of the time he was in the hospital, we could not hold him; we could only touch him to let him know we were there.

Never did I get used to the hospital routine. Never did I cease to hurt and pray as I walked down that long hallway for my last "glimpse" before surgery. The doctors tried to encourage us, telling us that this was just a way of life for the parents of a hydrocephalic. But it never became a "way of life" to me. I agonized with each disappointment and surgery, and I was thrilled with each step forward.

But I did praise God! I did, easily, give thanks. I did not thank God that Justin was hospitalized and hydrocephalic and needing surgery. The Bible commands us to give thanks *in* all things. And, in spite of our agony and our hurt, we didn't have to look very far to find things to be thankful for.

We could be thankful that God loved us; we could be thankful that God loved Justin—more than we—and in being confident of this love, we could trust Justin's life and health to God. We could be thankful that, for nine weeks, we were a "family of four." Medically speaking, we should never have had the opportunity to love our Justin.

We could be thankful that God had led us to such a compassionate church. God cared for us so tenderly through our ministers and fellow laymen. Orville spent countless hours in the hospital waiting room with us. Justin had a total of five surgeries, each lasting no less than two hours. Except for the one held on Sunday morning, Orville spent them all at our side. Even when we told him we didn't expect him to be there, he remained, giving us love and support. Not once during our long, difficult times did he criticize. He just loved us, as we were. We thanked God daily that He had led us to a church where the love of God was so prominent. *All* of our ministerial staff cared for us in a special way. We could, from our hearts, thank God that He was caring for us in the midst of our difficulty through our ministers and church.

We were so thankful for Jeff! God had even prepared his personality for what was to come at this period in his life. Never did he cry because we were leaving him again. He considered it a privilege to get to visit a friend and play at someone else's house. He would sometimes cry because we made him come home with us at the end of the day—I don't think we ever thanked God for that. And even though he begged to go with us to see Justin, I don't think he *ever* felt neglected because someone else had to care for him. He is very social and thoroughly enjoyed the attentions he received while we were in the hospital.

God beautifully cared for us through our Christian friends. We thanked Him for them daily. And God let us see how He was reaching out to others He loves through our situation—we could easily praise Him that good was coming from it.

We were new to our church and were overwhelmed by the love they heaped upon us. One day, a meal arrived just as Jerry was seeing off some out-of-town company and I was taking a long-distance phone call that had been holding while I said good-bye. I hardly knew the girl carrying in our evening meal. She walked into the home of strangers, bearing food and a smile—and was greeted by a group of people in the front yard yelling, "Go on in." When she walked in, as she held out the food she had so tenderly prepared, she was greeted by me, talking long-distance to my "sis," Sandra, crying my eyes out!

I felt so torn for the bearer of food; she stood, awkwardly, for a few moments, listening to me cry. Then she graciously deposited the food and slipped out before I got off the phone. I rushed to her to apologize at our next service—and found her rushing toward me! She spoke first: "I hope you'll forgive me for eavesdropping—but you'll never know how it blessed me. I just couldn't get over how you could praise God at a time like that! My faith was really strengthened to hear how He was caring for you." Needless to say, *she* strengthened my faith and reminded me that God was, indeed, using our "bad" circumstances to bring about His glory and goodness. And so it was, over and over again.

It was very hard for me to ask someone, again, daily—sometimes two or three times a day—to care for Jeff. And often, God would care for me so completely that I wouldn't have to. The phone would ring with a volunteer—"Can I keep Jeff for you while you're at the hospital?" Oh, God is so good! Of course, we can thank Him in our time of trouble!

And I could thank God for our families. Velda rushed to be by our side so often—I think she was there more than she was at home! Our family members cared for, loved, and supported us. The amazing thing is that no one criticized. They just loved. Maybe this amazes me because I have been critical of others. It is so easy for me to give advice and judge when I'm not the one going through the tough place. But God commands us just to love and not to judge—and our friends, ministers, and families did just that. I *had* to be thankful.

And I was so thankful that Jerry and I had each other. Some people have to face a tragedy alone; God had given us a radiant love that strengthened us. God is so good!

16

My Son—God's Son

For God so loved the world, that he gave his only begotten Son, that whosoever believeth in him should not perish, but have everlasting life (John 3:16).

Our little boy was in terrible pain! We visited daily and were ministered to by the nurses, many of them Christians who prayed for us and for Justin. But he continued to hurt—and we continued to hurt. The days got long; the weeks got long. He would appear better one day; the next day he would take a turn for the worse.

I never got used to the hospital. I never got used to the pain. Justin never had a blood test with me in the hallway that I didn't feel! Oh, I would gladly have traded places with him! I would gladly have hurt if he could have been made whole! He never got a shot that didn't hurt me.

Finally, in my desperation, I cried again to God, "God, it hurts so much to see him suffer!" And God tenderly wrapped His arms of love around me as He responded, "I know. I watched My Son suffer, too. I stood by helplessly, too. I understand, and I care." I realized, perhaps for the first time in my life, that He really *did* understand! I believe that God Almighty wept with me in compassionate love, for if we weep with another, understanding in a small way each other's sorrow, surely God—who knows the depths of our hurts—weeps, too!

I realized how very much God must love me. I was

losing one of my two sons—and was fighting it with all my might. I would gladly have suffered in Justin's place. Yet God loves *me* so much that He *willingly* gave His *only* Son! I had never *really* glimpsed at the depth of God's love before.

My concept of God the Father had been the Old Testament God of wrath—and I feared Him. I have been a Christian since I was five, but I was really only confident of Jesus' love. I could talk with Jesus, but I formally used "Thee" and "Thou" at the risk of angering God. I had often thought of Jesus' love—that He would willingly lay down His life and suffer for me. I don't mean to minimize the impact of that love—if it ever becomes unimportant that Jesus died for me, I'm off base. But now I've discovered a new dimension of God's love—the love of my Heavenly Father.

I never realized how deeply a parent could love a child, until I had my own. We would all gladly take our children's falls and fight their battles if we could keep them from having to hurt. We feel like striking back at those who wrongly strike out at our children. Nothing could hurt any deeper than to watch those we love suffer and be unable to do anything about it—or to watch those we love and believe in go out into sin and be unable to prevent it! We would gladly have their surgery and bear their pain *if*, in doing so, *their* bodies and hearts could be made whole.

Jesus was without sin—whole—perfect. It was so needless in human eyes for Him to suffer. Yet God *loves us* so much that He allowed it that we might be whole. That God could love ugly, sinful man so much really humbles me—and frees me—and makes me confident. I didn't have the power to keep Justin from suffering—to free his body of pain—to make him whole although I would *gladly* have suffered to make him whole. I would have given my life for his—IF . . . I *really* would have, but *only* under conditions of my own choosing.

God had that power. He could have spared His Son. But He loves me so much that He chose not to—even without the assurance that I would love Him in return. That staggers me! I lost a son to death—and I still can't comprehend the depth of that love!

You know, we owe God a healthy respect. When we use formal language out of respect and admiration for God, I believe He is pleased. But when we use it out of fear, I believe He hurts a little. I learned, through my experience, that God is more than Thee and Thou; He is "Daddy." I have never known what it was like to call someone "daddy." I have an Alton, and I have a Daboy, and no dad could have been better to me than those I adopted—but still I long for a "Daddy." Now I realize that I have had a "Daddy" all along—I just didn't recognize Him! If God is our Heavenly Father, He is our "Daddy."

Maybe I'm a little dense—after all, I've been a Christian since I was five. But I stand in awe at this concept! I am loved unconditionally by God, my Heavenly Father. He is, indeed, my "Daddy," whether or not I elect to know Him on that level! There is deep freedom in knowing that you are loved. I have gained a personal freedom because the love of my Father-God reached out and spoke to me through the deformed, helpless, hopeless little life of my son!

17

Wordless Tears

*And in the same way—by our faith—the Holy Spirit
helps us with our daily problems and in our praying.
For we don't even know what we should pray for, nor
how to pray as we should; but the Holy Spirit prays for
us with such feeling that it cannot be expressed in
words. And the Father who knows all hearts knows, of
course, what the Spirit is saying as he pleads for us in
harmony with God's own will* (Rom. 8:26-27, TLB).

The days were so full of pressure. We would visit our
baby to find him suffering, his body full of infection. In his
short life, he had had four major surgeries; now his body was
filled with an infection that, alone, can be fatal—spinal meningitis. Because of the infection, the doctors had to remove all
shunts; because he had no shunt, they had to "tap" his head
once each day to remove the fluid build-up. To do this, they
stuck a needle through his soft spot and removed anywhere
from one fourth to one cup of fluid. That meant daily in-
serting a needle into the portion of his brain that was the
largest—across the top of his head. During this time, we
could not hold him so we would sit with him, touch him, and
talk to him. The nurses ministered to us, and the non-
Christian nurses marveled at our strength and love. They
reached out to Justin, I think, because they knew we loved
him.

Our doctors were so conscientious and compassionate. One night we got a call from Dr. Weinberg about 9:30. He said, "I can't sleep without talking to you. I'm concerned about your baby. He might not make it through the night." Dr. Weinberg was off duty—he didn't even have to be at the hospital—but he cared enough to make a phone call.

Justin did live through the night—but during that week, we got *three* phone calls saying he was dying! Once his blood pressure jumped from 40 to 160 within one hour; an adult would have died under the circumstances. And because troubles seem to come in bundles, that same week, Jeff was ill with a virus, running a fever of 104. We had to have someone without children come to our home at a moment's notice to care for him, and we were torn in the depths of our soul each time we left our sick Jeff to be with Justin, and each time we left Justin to care for Jeff, realizing he might be in heaven before we could get back. But each time, God touched Justin to give him new life—and each time, the doctors shared their amazement at the strength of his little body.

I became so fearful. I was visiting Justin one night, feeling that he was at last getting better, when Dr. Weinberg walked in—again, around 9:30. I jumped, saying, "Oh, no! What's wrong? Why did they call you?" He responded, "I just wanted to see him before I went to bed—just to be sure he's okay." Have you ever had a doctor that cared that much? He made his routine calls at 9 a.m. He was off duty at 5:00. He had checked on Justin at 9:00, 12:00, 5:00—and now, at 9:30, he was returning—even when he didn't have to. Needless to say, I will always have a deep love and respect for that man.

My nerves could take no more! I jumped with fear each time the phone rang. Death was too close, and I was "running." Again, as became so normal for me during these days, I called on God. A friend had given us a record; one of the songs on it said, "When I think I'm goin' under, part the waters, Lord." I played that song and prayed that prayer, over and over, all day long. And do you know what happened? God parted the waters! I could bear no more; God sent a peace and a calm. Justin stabilized, Jeff recovered, and God ministered to my deepest need. I'm glad it says, "When I *think* I'm goin' under . . ." God cares about how we feel. He didn't "preach me a sermon." He tenderly parted the waters because my emotions needed it. He didn't quote promises to me that I knew were true—like "I can do all things . . ." He just, out of love for me, parted the waters because I needed a rest in the depth of my emotions. God's unspeakable love!

I soon realized that I feared life for Justin as much, even more, than I feared death. He began to improve; the infection began to clear up, but I remained fearful. I didn't want him to live as a vegetable. I didn't want him even to be trainable. I wanted God to either heal him completely or take him to heaven.

I was not alone in feeling that way. Mama, especially, prayed for nothing short of complete healing. Mama suffered polio as a child and lived her life in the aftermath of its destruction. She is brilliant and she has borne her handicap like a real champ. Rarely do you hear a complaint; usually you hear words of praise about how God has cared for her. But we never want those we love to bear what we ourselves have faced courageously. As she cried one day, she said, "I've had to go through life handicapped. It's terrible! I don't want him to live if he has to suffer as I have!"

And we never want those we love to make the same mistakes we make, even though we eventually see that those mistakes and problems are probably the reason for our growth. No matter how wrong it is, we treat people with handicaps as though they are "a little less than perfect." I think handicapped people who bear our persecution here (almost always unintentional and often unknown to us) must have a very special place prepared for them in heaven. They won't treat us as we've treated them, for there is no place for revengeful feelings in heaven. But surely there will be extra rewards for people like Mama who have been able to praise God in the midst of physical and mental problems, insulted by human persecution and misunderstanding.

Once I asked the surgeon, "Is there *really* any hope? Justin's chances were so slim to begin with. When you've had to tap daily to drain fluid, haven't you destroyed what brain tissue there is? Wouldn't spinal meningitis alone make him into a vegetable?"

He responded that he was very concerned about the things I had mentioned, but he just didn't know.

I replied, "Don't prolong the life of a vegetable. If there is no hope, don't medicate."

I hung up the phone guilty of murder! In my heart, I had just murdered my own son because I didn't want him to have to live a life of handicap! I had made myself into God! I will never forget the load of that guilt. I suffered with it and agonized for about a day. Then I asked God for forgiveness and called Dr. Bonner again. "That's not a decision I can make," I told him. "Do what is best for Justin." The wise Dr. Bonner replied that I didn't have to make that decision—when medically speaking it was really hopeless, he would feel free to cease abnormal medication. He assured me there was still indeed hope. Justin had proved himself to be a fighter far beyond the average hydrocephalic child. He also replied that usually One far greater than either of us makes that decision. Most likely we wouldn't have to face it. He assured me that there was hope—God had already shown us that in so many ways.

What a lesson! You know, if I were God, I'd be so angry with people like me who need constant reminders of His competency. Sign after sign, miracle after miracle, blessing after blessing—I had forgotten that God was God!

There will come a time when I'll forget again how adequate God is. Maybe with this record of how dynamically God cared for me, I can remember in future black times that God is still on the throne, He still loves me, and He is still working together for good—whether or not I can see it.

We learned the meaning of the verse that says when we don't know what to pray for, the Spirit prays for us, interpreting our words in accordance with the will of God. We prayed again that God's will would be done in the life of our son. Again we reminded ourselves that his destiny was in the hands of the only One who had the power to change things—in the hands of the Creator of all goodness who loved Justin more than we did—and who loved each of us far more than we loved each other or ourselves.

And Justin recovered! He started eating again! The IV came out. He grew and gained strength. We were able to hold him again! Just weeks after we had received three phone calls that he was dying, the doctors decided that he was strong enough for surgery and a new shunt. The meningitis healed remarkably. We might well not understand what we were going through, but we couldn't doubt that the Source of all love and of all wisdom had the life of our precious son in His arms.

Dr. Weinberg went on a well-earned vacation just as Justin began to improve. His replacement for two weeks was Dr. Voris, who had been on duty for him when Jeff was born. She was just as caring as Dr. Weinberg had been. Together she and Dr. Bonner scheduled Justin's fifth major surgery.

As Justin's condition improved, we began to feel the strain our family had been suffering—Jeff was able only to look at Justin through a window. He begged to see and hold his brother. We asked the nurses if Justin could go to the lobby; they responded that he shouldn't, but they probably "wouldn't notice" if Jeff came to his room for a while. They all agreed that Justin's brother needed the chance to love him. We tried to "sneak" a very happy Jeff into the hospital room where he held and loved his brother, oh, so tenderly! Those are moments Jeff will treasure all his life. The hospital staff recognized its importance and the nurses had to work hard to overlook the child we were "sneaking" in. Jeff announced loudly to *everyone* between the front door and the room: "I'm going to see my brother, Justin! I get to hold him in his room. I don't have to look through the window today."

Surgery day was set—and, as the day approached, I began to feel that this would be the end. Suddenly I realized that I wanted another picture! When Dr. Bonner made his late night call the evening before surgery—about 11:00—we mentioned that we wished we had taken Justin's picture with Jeff. We mentioned that we would like to "sneak" Justin to the lobby for a few minutes. He said, "By all means, do! I'll make an order to that effect! Let his brother see him and love him!" Before we got to the hospital at 8:00 that morning, Dr. Bonner had been there; on top of Justin's chart, in large print, were orders that said, "Allow Justin to go to lobby for pictures!" I can't begin to tell you what those pictures mean to me! This was the last time we saw Justin coherent and wide-eyed! And I have my picture—all because God sent us a surgeon who realized that where there is handicap, there is a whole family with emotional needs! God indeed answered our prayers!

We didn't know what was best for Justin. We didn't know how to pray. We didn't know whether to pray for his healing or for God to take him to heaven. We knew things seemed hopeless. Finally, we simply claimed God's promise that the Holy Spirit would pray for us, and turned our wordless tears over to God.

18

Justin Goes Home to God

Yea, though I walk through the valley of the shadow of death, I will fear no evil: for thou art with me; thy rod and thy staff, they comfort me (Ps. 23:4).

I carried my baby back down the hallway to his room. With about an hour to spend with him before they prepared him for surgery, I became aware as I walked down that hallway that a deep sense of peace walked with me. I sat with Justin in my arms, loving him and taking in his love, for about an hour—in perfect peace. This is so rare for me. I'm such a hyper person that I can't sit *anywhere* and do nothing for more than 10 minutes. But that morning, God just wrapped His loving arms around Justin and me both, and surrounded us with His peace.

I wouldn't allow my thoughts to surface into words, but I knew I was holding my baby for the last time. Rather than panicking and fighting for his life and arguing with God that this was unfair, or running from Justin because I was afraid that if I loved more I would hurt more, I sat surrounded by a *wall* of peace and love and acceptance and contentment. I recognized God's strength, because it was the same presence that ushered me out of the delivery room on the day of Justin's birth. Everything was *okay*. Someone bigger than life was in control. Whatever happened would be *okay*. I could just sit, relax, and enjoy loving my son for the last time on earth.

For a few moments, Justin and I together tasted of heaven. His battle was almost ended, and the God of the universe held us both securely in His arms. It was, indeed, the very presence of God that allowed me the luxury of loving my son that morning.

I knew that, if God chose, Justin could be wheeled out of surgery, completely healed and completely whole. I also knew that, if God chose, Justin could be healed completely without that last surgery. But then God could choose to take Justin to heaven, the only permanent healing. And *any* of those choices would be *okay* because the God that was to make them loved Justin and loved Jeff and loved Jerry and loved me enough that He *would make the best decision in all of our interests. With God, all things work together for good.* I don't know how He does it, but I know that He does. I realized, as I sat there holding and loving, that I was treading on holy ground! There were three of us who sat there for about an hour—I was holding my baby for the last time, and Jesus was sheltering us both under His wings of love. Jerry arrived shortly before they wheeled Justin in to surgery; he commented later that he felt that Divine Presence, too.

I'll never forget Justin's eyes as I placed him on his crib to get his preoperative shot. How hard it was to put him down—to allow that solitude to end! He looked at me and jumped, crying, as if to say, "You've just been loving me—now you're letting them hurt me again!" And I hurt with him again, but I knew in my heart that he wouldn't have to hurt much longer and that God understood how I felt.

They wheeled him down that long hallway again. It would seem that by the fifth time we had watched him as he disappeared behind those closed doors, it would become routine. But it never could. Each time we prayed that Jesus would go with him; each time we knew that the Divine Healer was guiding the hands of the surgeon; each time it hurt a little deeper because we loved a little more; each time we waited anxiously for the surgeon to reappear; each time the surgery lasted longer than it should have; and each time we began to worry and walk the floor. Each time we met new people in the lobby and shared together our hopes and fears and faith. Each time we made it through the ordeal without an ounce of strength to spare, but each time we had the strength we needed. The last was no different. I had a deep sense of peace; I didn't worry through that surgery, even though I was anxious. I expected the surgeon to tell us Justin hadn't survived the operating table, but oh, I prayed that he would! I knew I had held him for the last time—I knew it was *okay*—but perhaps . . .

The doctor returned to tell us that he was in recovery and that he had survived the operation. Things were going quite well, and he would be back in his room shortly where we could see him. I told myself that I had just imagined my sense that he wouldn't make it—that he would be okay—that I was just afraid he would die and was trying, again, to detach myself.

When we saw Justin, he seemed all right. His nurse, who was new to us, was unusually quiet. She didn't leave his side, and she checked his vital signs more often than after previous surgeries. Normally there is a constant watch for an hour after surgery; the hour came and went but the constant watch went on. Nothing was wrong, but things weren't right either. We watched and waited; finally, still apprehensive, we went home for the night.

When Jerry arrived at the hospital early the next morning, he found Justin's room full of doctors, nurses, and equipment. When he didn't call to report at the usual time, I called the hospital to check on Justin, thinking Jerry was tied up in a meeting. Jerry was still there, and Justin was in oxygen; he had pneumonia. Deep inside I knew this was coming, but I didn't want it to be! The days dragged on; his condition remained the same. His vitals were stabilized, but the pneumonia didn't clear; he made no response to his stimulations. A flashlight shined in his eyes caused no reaction in his pupils.

But the long, discouraging days were filled with the touch of God! Doctors, nurses, patients, parents, friends all ministered to us. And in spite of the seemingly hopeless diagnosis, the staff fervently worked to save Justin's life.

Hospital routines continued to be a big part of our lives. It seemed that so many of the people I met during those hospital visits were beautiful. But when you spend time in a hospital, you come face-to-face with a lot of ugliness, too. There were little girls admitted who had been the victims of incest; children who had been abused; children who had been neglected and forgotten. One baby died the day before Justin did; he was 7 months old and had never left the hospital. During our 2½-month stay, when either Jerry or I were there off and on all day long, we never once saw his parents! Oh, how I wished that child had someone to love him! It seemed as though life would be cruel to him even if he survived. He had a doctor who kept him alive by machines. One day while we were there, the little fellow was sitting by the nurses' station without his oxygen. We were thrilled until we heard that the doctor had decided that "blue" was his "normal" color. About that time, he began to gasp for breath! While I watched, the nurse called a "Blue Alert," rushed him to his room, and we witnessed this baby being brought back to life in the midst of confusion—all staff doctors, nurses, and machines rushing to save him.

He died early the next morning. We learned that, after seven months of keeping him alive, the doctor had finally decided that if he couldn't live outside of oxygen, he couldn't live. We heard later that his insurance had paid its maximum benefit the day before that decision was made. You can see why I praise God for *our* doctors!

Jerry and I watched, speechless, hurting! The poor little boy had been cheated! Such a hopeless little life; now he wasn't even allowed to die with dignity! Realizing that Justin, too, was nearing death, we called our doctors that night, reminding them of our request that he not be placed on "Blue Alert." He had the right to live, and we wanted to do everything within our power to make his life worthwhile and happy; but he also had the right to die with dignity and in peace rather than confusion. We found that our doctors had already honored our wishes and had noted on Justin's chart that the nurses were to call no alert when the time came. After we had done everything reasonable to help Justin, we had to leave his healing in the hands of a greater power. If God chose to take Justin to heaven for healing, his homegoing should be glorious. It should be a quiet, spiritual, peaceful time. Yes, we knew there would be tears—but not confusion. We wanted to be with him when he died, but most of all we wanted him to be allowed to run to the arms of Jesus without another earthly battle. And even though we knew it was coming—and soon—we still prayed that God would see fit to heal him instead. Where there is life and love, there must remain hope.

We realized we were being watched closely as our child suffered. New children would be admitted, and we would hear from their parents: "It is easy to see that Justin is one of the favorites around here." They were not words of jealousy, though; they were words of love. That amazes me. Justin got a new roommate—a sweet little girl with Christian parents who sensed God's presence and talked to us of faith. We prayed constantly that God would use us to show His love—to radiate back, in some measure, the goodness we were receiving from His hand. Our lives are far from perfect, but

God uses imperfect people to show His perfect love. We felt a deep bond with the nurses and felt they loved Justin partly because we did! They tried harder because they knew we cared, loved him, and appreciated their efforts. God was to show me, though, that there was more to it than our love!

We had prayed that God would love through Justin and bring good from his life. We didn't have any idea how He could do it. We knew He could be glorified through our attitude, and He gave us an attitude of praise during those months. We felt Justin was special, but what parent could feel otherwise about his child? Our concept of God really being lifted up and glorified, though, was limited to our vision of total human healing. We felt "we" were the key to God being glorified in Justin. Our friends told their friends about Justin, and people who didn't even know us prayed for us. Good came from all over the world, and people everywhere let us know that their lives had been touched because of Justin. People I have seen, even years later, would say, "Oh, you're Justin's mother! We've prayed for you, but I didn't know who you were."

God used *all* those prayers to bless us during our tough times, but God is so much bigger than we gave Him credit for. He really didn't even need *us* to make Justin's life worthwhile. The Bible says that if man doesn't praise Him, the rocks will cry out! And the love of God literally filled the helpless, hopeless little body of a child named Justin; and from what the devil meant for bad, *God made good!*

The testimony of a nurse backed up that belief. It was Friday the 13th. Jerry had about a two-hour break for lunch before his next appointment. I left him with Jeff while I slipped off to be with Justin. I just wanted to sit with him; I could slip my hand under the oxygen tent to touch him and hold his hand. If I couldn't hold him, I had to touch him to let him know we were still there pulling for him and loving him.

He was lifeless; the nurse came in to give him his shot, and I said, "Kick her, Justin! Don't let her get away with that!" She responded, "Oh, how I wish he would!" He didn't even flinch as the needle went in; I hurt for him, but I hurt even more knowing that he couldn't respond.

I was about to leave when Dr. Bonner walked in to check him, about 1:30 in the afternoon. He asked me to step out for a few moments while he examined Justin; then to wait to talk to him. He had been there for just moments when Dr. Voris walked in. They talked to me in the hallway for a few moments. Both said things didn't look good—Justin was a very sick baby. I said, "But his vitals are good! Is he as sick now as when his blood pressure was jumping around?" I would grasp at every hope while there was life! They responded that they really couldn't tell—Justin was a fighter, and he had surprised them many times—but he was, at least, no better than he had been weeks earlier when we had received our "death" calls. Then came the final blow: Dr. Bonner was leaving on vacation for two weeks; Dr. Voris was off duty at 5:00; Dr Weinberg would not return until Monday.

As they walked away, panic set in! Then I realized . . . God cares about the little things! It's important to me that, when he dies, there be a doctor I have confidence in on duty! He'll be gone by 5:00—or he'll be alive on Monday when Dr. Weinberg returns. I convinced myself that he would be alive on Monday before I walked back into his room.

The nurse was listening to his lungs and let me hear the pneumonia. The congestion was unbelievable to my un-educated ear. I had no doubts; I called Jerry to cancel his appointments and come to the hospital. We sat with him for three hours, every few minutes telling ourselves he'd make it, and constantly looking for signs of life and health.

The entire hospital seemed to know that Justin was dying. This was strange, because his vitals were fine—better than they had been. He was under light oxygen but wasn't responding to treatment. He had pneumonia, but not that bad. Yet everyone knew. Every few minutes someone would drop in to love him and to love us.

A nurse came in and exclaimed: "You're Justin's parents! I heard you were here, and I just had to meet you. I don't know what your son has, but he's touched my life! We all fight over who gets to hold Justin. I win because I'm the loudest and —I don't know how to describe it—he's filling a need in my life. I just sit and hold him, and something happens. I don't know what it is, but there's a need there, and when I hold him, it's filled!"

I was, of course, deeply touched, but I really didn't understand. I responded, "You'd just have to love a baby!"

She replied, "No. I've worked here for six years, and this is the first time I've ever been touched by a life. He's different. He's got something!"

It dawned on me! I'm a little slow, but it began to sink in! We had prayed that God would shine His love through Justin—*and He did!* I felt speechless! I didn't know how to tell her she had been touched by God! Finally I stammered something about how much God loves us to have given His only Son. But, you know, God really didn't even need me around to bring good through Justin's life! Justin was too pure to resist God, and He can work through *any* life that will allow Him to.

Many questions about how this could be have filled my mind. Could God have used Justin if we hadn't dedicated him and let go? Or do we inhibit God's work by being selfish and refusing to allow Him the opportunity to shine? One thing is certain—God's love, through a baby named Justin, reached out to touch the soul of one that He loved! She didn't know what had touched her, but she knew she had received. It was

God's love, not ours, that was responsible for *all* the goodness! We had merely been privileged to see it and rejoice.

A nurse we had grown to love walked in to check on Justin. She had ministered to us in the past; we said, "It must be hard to work here, so close to death." She responded that it had been; she had decided to resign because it hurt so to watch children suffer and die, but her mother had reminded her that with children, there is no question: "To be absent from the body is to be present with the Lord!" With that assurance, she could care for the children, knowing that if human efforts proved unsuccessful, the children became whole.

She removed the oxygen from Justin to examine him; it was about 4:30. He waved an arm at her—and I shouted for joy! Jerry and I gathered around, so thrilled to see movement in a child that had for so long remained motionless. Then we discovered that the nurse was not joyful. She was checking his pulse and replacing the oxygen. A therapist came in to give him a lung treatment for his pneumonia; as he left he pulled the curtain to leave us alone with our baby.

Within moments, Justin was gone—so peacefully and calmly! Perhaps his arms had been reaching out to receive the embrace of Jesus! As we said good-bye, tears streaming down our faces, Jerry said, "Honey, a little bit of us just went to heaven."

We were alone only for a few moments. And then the great God who cares about the little things in our life sent in two beautiful Christian nurses to minister to us until the doctor could return to pronounce him dead. The nurses joined us in a prayer of thanksgiving that our child was now completely whole, healthy, free of pain, and that we would be able to go on and face our responsibilities here on earth with a new outlook on life because we had been touched by God through a child named Justin.

The great God who cares about the little things in our lives had made sure that a doctor we respected was on duty, and we had been alerted to be there. It was a quiet, beautiful moment when Justin slipped into heaven, not spoiled by machines and noise and blue alerts. And I didn't see it happen, but I know that the heavens were opened and the angels were rejoicing as a child named Justin, a beautiful baby who fought against all hope on earth, in a moment—in the twinkling of an eye—became totally free of pain and totally healed and totally whole forever. I believe the room was filled with angels singing praises as, once again, death seemed the victor over life—but new life won!

I believe Gammy and Daboy were there to welcome their special baby, and that became such a comfort to me. Rather than resenting the fact that another life of one I loved had been lost to me temporarily through death, I was comforted to know that those I love were there to love him for me until we would meet again. I don't know how people change and grow in heaven, but the Bible tells us that we will know as we are known; so I'll know him, and he'll know me, and the plan of life that God has for us there will be far better than the limited life our imaginations here can comprehend. He's healed and won't suffer anymore—and we'll meet again because of the blood of Jesus!

Dr. Voris arrived to examine Justin and officially pronounce him dead. She looked down into a face, now peaceful at last, and said, "Well, Justin, you were a fighter!" And I still beam with pride when I remember those words! I pray that I can defy the odds set for my life, as he did. She volunteered to observe the autopsy the next day and call us with the report, even though she was off duty. She told us that we could stay with the body as long as we liked, but kindly reminded us that Justin was no longer in need of us—and Jeff was!

109

It dawned on us that since Justin was gone, we didn't need to be there either. We began the "long" trip across town to tell Jeff that his brother was in heaven. As I started up the motor, the great God who cares about the little things sent a song through the car radio—"It Will Be Worth It All when We See Jesus." And God whispered to my soul that the words were true. We seem to think a worthwhile life is one that accomplishes something and acquires its share of the good things—yet we asked God to use Justin's life. At least one soul has testified to being saved as a direct result of Justin's life—perhaps others were—and numerous lives were touched. Perhaps we all need a new set of values. "It *will* be worth it all when we see Jesus."

That evening, we received a call from Dr. Bonner. Dr. Voris had called him with the news, and he called us before leaving on vacation to give his condolences and reassure us. He said, "I know it is best because his chances were so slim, but I know you love him, and I'm sorry it had to be this way. What Justin had should not happen again. I guess his little body had just fought all it could! I thought he was strong enough to pull through another surgery—you never know—but I think his body just couldn't take any more."

Dr. Voris called us the next day after observing the autopsy with some surprising news. She said, "I don't even know what to put on Justin's death certificate. Medically speaking, there is no reason why he should have died. He had just a couple of tiny patches of pneumonia in his lungs, but not enough to kill him. The only thing I can say is that his body just couldn't fight any longer."

In a normal death, that news would be frustrating—but in this case, it was just a part of God's miracle. The pneumonia had been God's way of getting us to the hospital, and we really wanted to be there when he died. And the "no medical reason" said to me that he really didn't "die," as we normally use the word—Jesus simply came and took him home. He had suffered enough. He had been through enough pain. He had fought long and hard and defied the odds over and over again and surprised the doctors over and over again. He didn't have a chance, yet he fought long and hard. He hung in there! He didn't let go and give up! Finally God said to him, "It's all over! Come home and rest."

What a glorious way to go! Pneumonia didn't kill him! Jesus just came to take him home.

It's always hard when a child or young person dies; but if we belong to Jesus, we need "fear no evil," for He is with us just as surely as He is with the one we love who has gone to heaven. The Psalmist's words are beautifully true, whether it is you who are facing death personally or whether one you love has been taken home: "Yea, though I walk through the valley of the shadow of death, I will *fear no evil: for thou art with me;* thy rod and thy staff *they comfort me.*"

When the actual time came to face Justin's death, I was at perfect peace! We need never fear when Jesus is with us—we need only open our lives to receive His comfort.

19

Celebration of Praise

But Jesus said, "Let the little children come to me, and don't prevent them. For of such is the Kingdom of Heaven" (Matt. 19:14, TLB).

It is unusual to have a funeral service for a small baby, but Justin's life had been so involved in the lives of other people that we couldn't just "walk away." We requested a memorial service of praise in his honor.

I had always thought of a mortician as being a morbid person, but I learned that a mortician who is really doing his job has a calling from God just as a minister does. The mortician very tactfully helped us with our decisions. He could sense when we were unable to decide and would tactfully change the subject until a better opportunity came up. When he asked us if we wanted to show the body, we had mixed emotions. I had never wanted to view a body; I had said my good-bye in the hospital, so I didn't really think I wanted the body viewed; but I knew that my family who came for the service would want to see him. Even though this is not a custom that I'm fond of, I wanted to respect the wishes of the others I love. Because Justin's autopsy centered in his brain, however, he was skeptical about whether this would be possible. He told us that the people performing an autopsy usually did a good job of "butchering" and that he would try, but couldn't promise that the body could be shown.

Early the next morning, we got a call from the mortician.

Jerry talked while I listened in, and he did not realize I was on the phone. His words were so tender! "I'm so happy to tell you that I'll be able to show the body. They did an unusually neat job during the autopsy, and you have a very beautiful baby! I sensed that your wife really *did* want to see him again, and I'm so happy that she'll have that chance." This tender attitude carried through in our every connection with him. And I really *did* need to see Justin again. I just didn't know it until the time came.

We got another call that the body could be viewed. This "formality" of death is something I had never understood. When friends had died, I had begged out of it as often as I could. Now I was to see the body of my own son. That little body that had been wracked with pain for most of his life, and especially for the last nine weeks, was a beautiful, healthy, whole baby—face radiant and free of pain, looking asleep. Oh, how I agonized! "God, why did it have to be this way? He's so healthy! He could have made it! How could such an outwardly beautiful child have so many things wrong? Life is so full of inequities. It can't be true! He looks so alive." Then I realized that this was the first time I had seen Justin when he was truly free of pain and truly alive! Oh, it hurt— but it was so necessary. In looking back, I have learned many lessons from the "morbid" experience of viewing the body. I'm very thankful that I didn't cheat myself out of that experience—and that we had a mortician who was sensitive enough to read past my words into my grief to help bring about an experience I needed.

We had Justin dressed in his red and white playsuit with his white booties. He wore his red, white, and blue cap. He had slept and played that way many times, and he looked so alive now. We had a hard time deciding how to dress him— considering new, dressy clothes. Jerry selected the outfit Justin wore so often; and when Alton arrived, he commented,

"I've always thought children should be buried the way they play. That's what's most natural for them, and I'm sure they play in heaven. I'm glad you chose those clothes." Beside him in the casket stood his little blue bunny, our Easter gift to him that served in the hospital as his "color stimulation" and that he had learned to touch and hold while at home. Alton and Margie had given him a Bible, and it stood open to their inscription, "Jesus said, Suffer little children, and forbid them not, to come unto me: for of such is the kingdom of heaven." We talked of how appropriate it was. They had no idea he was facing surgery and heaven when they wrote it, but they had been led to it as "right" for Justin. And our thoughtful mortician had chosen that as the page to display! God took care of all the details.

We went to the florist to order his flowers. I had been doing pretty well, but when the florist asked us what we would like the banner to say, I burst into tears, uncontrollably, and was unable to answer. I knew . . . but I couldn't speak. Even though we hadn't discussed it, Jerry said the very words that just wouldn't come out of my mouth: "Our Heaven Baby."

As we headed for the car, Jeff grabbed me around the neck and began hugging me and saying, "Don't cry, Mommy! Justin's okay! He's in heaven! He's with Jesus! Justin's all right! He's not sick anymore! He doesn't hurt anymore! Don't cry, Mommy!" What a simple faith a child has! Is it any wonder that Jesus loved children and praised their faith! We explained that we cried for ourselves, not for Justin—that we would miss him, and we hurt. But again we realized that God had blessed us greatly with our son Jeff and was answering our prayers that Justin's life would have a positive effect rather than a negative one on him.

Following a private graveside service for our immediate family, our friends and loved ones gathered for a memorial service of praise in memory of Justin—a perfect way to say, "Good-bye." We needed to share our praise to God for carrying us through the past few months and to say to our friends that what they had witnessed in us had been the goodness of God, that we were very ordinary people who served a very extraordinary God. Our friends ministered to us in our sorrow and rejoiced with us in Justin's total healing. Justin had a dynamic, happy homegoing!

When the autopsy report finally arrived, we learned that Justin's brain had been severely damaged and the hydrocephalus occurred shortly after conception, during the third week of development. Probably this was caused by a virus, not strong enough for me to realize I had it but destructive to the fetus. Medically speaking, he didn't have the brain capacity to see and to follow my movement around the room because that portion of his brain was destroyed completely. This served months later as a reminder to us that God had, indeed, healed our son and allowed us to love him on earth for 4½ short months. I shall be forever grateful to God for His healing touch on the life of my son.

A friend of mine who lost a baby said she learned so much through her experience that if she could choose it, she would do it the same way again. I can't honestly say that.

My little Justin, if I could choose your life, you would be whole and healthy and free of pain and live an easy, full life here on earth. But it's not that way. God has chosen to take you home . . . to His home.

> . . . help me then remember
> how Your Son suffered
> and You stood by
> watching
> agonizing watching
> waiting

to bring all suffering to an end
forever
on a day
yet to be . . .*

Justin, Heaven's Baby, you are my very priceless, precious treasure in heaven. Heaven has always been a special
place to me, but now a little bit of my heart lives there. One
of these mornings, we will have a beautiful, joyful reunion.
In the meantime, please know that, along with all the other
goodness your life inspired, your life has made your mother
a better person. I wouldn't have chosen your life this way, but
I am blessed, indeed, to have shared it.

----
*Joseph Bayly, *A Psalm in Children's Hospital.*

Epilogue

To every thing there is a season . . . a time to be born, and a time to die . . . a time to weep, and a time to laugh; a time to mourn, and a time to dance (Eccles. 3:1-2, 4).

The laws of the universe apply to our personal lives. "What goes up must come down." When we live on a high, a low will follow—the higher the high, the lower the low. Oh, yes! And sunshine *always* follows rain.

We had lived on a high during Justin's lifetime. The low had to follow, and when it did, we couldn't handle it. We were so spoiled by God's special blessings that we had learned to think of strength and peace as God's only way of doing things. We refused to believe that it was "normal" to mourn. As we tried to muster up our praise that had flowed so freely the past few months, we faced something that was really worse than packing away clothes for a baby who never came home: packing away—for the second time—clothes for a baby who had finally come home and worn them and been loved by us. We thought that since God had shown us that He was in our situation, we didn't have the right to "hurt" because we knew God's will had been done.

Our sense of direction had been changed overnight. We were at a loss as to what to do with ourselves. We received strong support from our family and friends, but we didn't know how to mourn. It is too often the case that we "run" from grief, and Jerry ran back—to alcohol! A much greater tragedy followed the one we had just completed.

In the months that followed, in spite of extensive counseling and prayers, our home was broken. Jerry and I were divorced. A deep depression came over me. Satan told me that the divorce had destroyed God's goodness brought through Justin, and I carried a heavy load of guilt which compounded my grief.

In a very difficult walk through my depression, I learned some important lessons. God's glory shines just as brightly through our tears, although we often cannot see it until the tears of sorrow are gone.

When we refuse to spend time mourning a loss, we carry that loss with us for the rest of our lives. If we are to be free to live again, we must mourn. Now that my mourning has ended, I have discovered the quality of love I carry for Justin still shines; a mother's love lasts forever.

Jesus stands ready to weep and mourn with us; when we are alone, we have One who will share our heartache.

Time is a great healer, and God has richly blessed me with a new job and a new life. Jeff and I have discovered that, with God's help, one parent and one child make a family. We miss the times we were a family of four, but we are free to enjoy life as it is now. The morning is again dawning in our lives, and we see bright rays of sunshine—just as He promised.

Writing these pages was a major step in my healing process; and responding to God's call to write for Him has given me renewed purpose. I feel deeply honored to bear the title "author." Had I written this book before my life was complicated by divorce, loneliness, and depression, it would have given an unrealistic picture of God's protective grace. As I look back, God was not merely protecting me by His goodness during Justin's lifetime; He was building my faith and strength so I would hold on in the years to come. He knew that, if I was to survive a broken home, I would need His special touch and insight to remind me of His faithfulness.

It is my deepest prayer that, as you read this, you will find strength through Justin's story to trust God through the trials of your own life. Whether we can see His handiwork clearly or not, God's promises are true; and God—the God of integrity—*always* keeps His promises!